Excel 2002
Simplified®

Visual

From
maranGraphics®

&

Hungry Minds™

Best-Selling Books • Digital Downloads • e-books • Answer Networks •
e-Newsletters • Branded Web Sites • e-learning

New York, NY ♦ Cleveland, OH ♦ Indianapolis, IN

Excel 2002 Simplified®

Published by
Hungry Minds, Inc.
909 Third Avenue
New York, NY 10022
www.hungryminds.com

Copyright© 2002 by maranGraphics Inc.
5755 Coopers Avenue
Mississauga, Ontario, Canada
L4Z 1R9

Library of Congress Control Number: 2001096758
ISBN: 0-7645-3589-7
Printed in the United States of America
10 9 8 7 6 5 4 3 2 1
1K/QV/RS/QR/MG

Distributed in the United States by Hungry Minds, Inc.
Distributed by CDG Books Canada Inc. for Canada; by Transworld Publishers Limited in the United Kingdom; by IDG Norge Books for Norway; by IDG Sweden Books for Sweden; by IDG Books Australia Publishing Corporation Pty. Ltd. for Australia and New Zealand; by TransQuest Publishers Pte Ltd. for Singapore, Malaysia, Thailand, Indonesia, and Hong Kong; by Gotop Information Inc. for Taiwan; by ICG Muse, Inc. for Japan; by Intersoft for South Africa; by Eyrolles for France; by International Thomson Publishing for Germany, Austria and Switzerland; by Distribuidora Cuspide for Argentina; by LR International for Brazil; by Galileo Libros for Chile; by Ediciones ZETA S.C.R. Ltda. for Peru; by WS Computer Publishing Corporation, Inc. for the Philippines; by Contemporanea de Ediciones for Venezuela; by Express Computer Distributors for the Caribbean and West Indies; by Micronesia Media Distributor, Inc. for Micronesia; by Chips Computadoras S.A. de C.V. for Mexico; by Editorial Norma de Panama S.A. for Panama; by American Bookshops for Finland.
For corporate orders, please call maranGraphics at 800-469-6616 or fax 905-890-9434.
For general information on Hungry Minds' products and services, please contact our Customer Care Department within the U.S. at 800-762-2974, outside the U.S. at 317-572-3993 or fax 317-572-4002.
For sales inquiries and reseller information, including discounts, premium and bulk quantity sales, and foreign-language translations, please contact our Customer Care Department at 800-434-3422, fax 317-572-4002, or write to Hungry Minds, Inc., Attn: Customer Care Department, 10475 Crosspoint Boulevard, Indianapolis, IN 46256.
For information on licensing foreign or domestic rights, please contact our Sub-Rights Customer Care Department at 212-844-5000.
For information on using Hungry Minds' products and services in the classroom or for ordering examination copies, please contact our Educational Sales Department at 800-434-2086 or fax 317-572-4005.
For press review copies, author interviews, or other publicity information, please contact our Public Relations department at 317-572-3168 or fax 317-572-4168.
For authorization to photocopy items for corporate, personal, or educational use, please contact maranGraphics at the address above.

Trademark Acknowledgments

Permissions

Hungry Minds™ is a trademark of Hungry Minds, Inc.

U.S. Corporate Sales	**U.S. Trade Sales**
Contact maranGraphics at (800) 469-6616 or fax (905) 890-9434.	Contact Hungry Minds at (800) 434-3422 or fax (317) 572-4002.

Some comments from our readers...

"Compliments To The Chef!! Your books are extraordinary! Or, simply put, Extra-Ordinary, meaning way above the rest! THANK YOU THANK YOU THANK YOU! for creating these. I buy them for friends, family, and colleagues."
— *Christine J. Manfrin (Castle Rock, CO)*

"What fantastic teaching books you have produced! Congratulations to you and your staff. You deserve the Nobel prize in Education in the Software category. Thanks for helping me to understand computers."
— *Bruno Tonon (Melbourne, Australia)*

"I was introduced to maranGraphics about four years ago and YOU ARE THE GREATEST THING THAT EVER HAPPENED TO INTRODUCTORY COMPUTER BOOKS!"
— *Glenn Nettleton (Huntsville, AL)*

"I'm a grandma who was pushed by an 11-year-old grandson to join the computer age. I found myself hopelessly confused and frustrated until I discovered the Visual series. I'm no expert by any means now, but I'm a lot further along than I would have been otherwise. Thank you!"
— *Carol Louthain (Logansport, IN)*

"Thank you, thank you, thank you...for making it so easy for me to break into this high-tech world. I now own four of your books. I recommend them to anyone who is a beginner like myself. Now...if you could just do one for programming VCRs, it would make my day!"
— *Gay O'Donnell (Calgary, Alberta, Canada)*

"I write to extend my thanks and appreciation for your books. They are clear, easy to follow, and straight to the point. Keep up the good work!"
— *Seward Kollie (Dakar, Senegal)*

"Thank you for making it a lot easier to learn the basics."
— *Allan Black (Woodlawn, Ontario, Canada)*

"Your books are superior! An avid reader since childhood, I've consumed literally tens of thousands of books, a significant quantity in the learning/teaching category. Your series is the most precise, visually appealing, and compelling to peruse. Kudos!"
— *Margaret Chmilar (Edmonton, Alberta, Canada)*

"I just want to tell you how much I, a true beginner, really enjoy your books and now understand a lot more about my computer and working with Windows. I'm 51 and a long time out of the classroom, but these books make it easier for me to learn. Hats off to you for a great product."
— *William K. Rodgers (Spencer, NC)*

"I would like to take this time to thank you and your company for producing great and easy to learn products. I bought two of your books from a local bookstore, and it was the best investment I've ever made!"
— *Jeff Eastman (West Des Moines, IA)*

"I would like to take this time to compliment maranGraphics on creating such great books. Thank you for making it clear. Keep up the good work."
— *Kirk Santoro (Burbank, CA)*

"I have to praise you and your company on the fine products you turn out. Thank you for creating books that are easy to follow. Keep turning out those quality books."
— *Gordon Justin (Brielle, NJ)*

"Over time, I have bought a number of your 'Read Less-Learn More' books. For me, they are THE way to learn anything easily. I learn easiest using your method of teaching."
— *José A. Mazón (Cuba, NY)*

maranGraphics is a family-run business located near Toronto, Canada.

At **maranGraphics**, we believe in producing great computer books—one book at a time.

Each maranGraphics book uses the award-winning communication process that we have been developing over the last 25 years. Using this process, we organize screen shots, text and illustrations in a way that makes it easy for you to learn new concepts and tasks.

We spend hours deciding the best way to perform each task, so you don't have to! Our clear, easy-to-follow screen shots and instructions walk you through each task from beginning to end.

Our detailed illustrations go hand-in-hand with the text to help reinforce the information. Each illustration is a labor of love—some take up to a week to draw!

We want to thank you for purchasing what we feel are the best computer books money can buy. We hope you enjoy using this book as much as we enjoyed creating it!

Sincerely,

The Maran Family

Please visit us on the Web at:
www.maran.com

Credits

Author:
Ruth Maran

Copy Development Director:
Wanda Lawrie

**Copy Editing
and Screen Captures:**
Roxanne Van Damme
Stacey Morrison

Project Manager:
Judy Maran

Editors:
Teri Lynn Pinsent
Norm Schumacher
Megan Kirby

Layout Artist and Illustrator:
Treena Lees

Illustrators:
Russ Marini
Steven Schaerer

Screen Artist and Illustrator:
Darryl Grossi

Indexer:
Teri Lynn Pinsent

Permissions Coordinator:
Jennifer Amaral

**Senior Vice President
and Publisher, Hungry Minds
Technology Publishing Group:**
Richard Swadley

**Publishing Director,
Hungry Minds Technology
Publishing Group:**
Barry Pruett

**Editorial Support,
Hungry Minds Technology
Publishing Group:**
Jennifer Dorsey
Sandy Rodrigues
Lindsay Sandman

Post Production:
Robert Maran

Acknowledgments

Thanks to the dedicated staff of maranGraphics, including
Jennifer Amaral, Roderick Anatalio, Darryl Grossi,
Kelleigh Johnson, Megan Kirby, Wanda Lawrie,
Treena Lees, Cathy Lo, Jill Maran, Judy Maran, Robert Maran,
Ruth Maran, Russ Marini, Teri Lynn Pinsent, Steven Schaerer,
Norm Schumacher, Raquel Scott, Roxanne Van Damme
and Paul Whitehead.

Finally, to Richard Maran who originated the easy-to-use
graphic format of this guide. Thank you for your
inspiration and guidance.

Table of Contents

Table of Contents

CHAPTER 7

PRINT YOUR WORKSHEETS

CHAPTER 8

WORK WITH MULTIPLE WORKSHEETS

CHAPTER 9

WORK WITH CHARTS

CHAPTER 1

GETTING STARTED

Are you ready to begin using Microsoft Excel 2002? This chapter will help you get started.

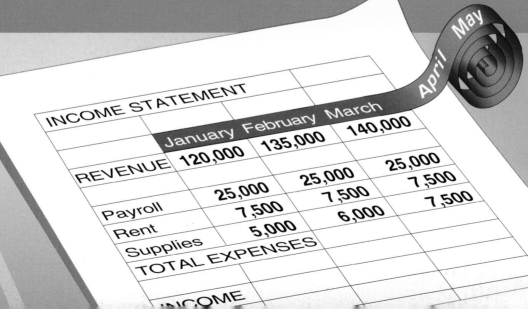

INCOME STATEMENT	January	February	March	April	May
REVENUE	120,000	135,000	140,000		
Payroll	25,000	25,000	25,000		
Rent	7,500	7,500	7,500		
Supplies	5,000	6,000	7,500		
TOTAL EXPENSES					
INCOME					

INTRODUCTION TO EXCEL

Excel is a spreadsheet program you can use to organize, analyze and attractively present data such as a budget or sales report.

Edit and Format Data

Excel allows you to efficiently enter, edit and format data in a worksheet. You can quickly enter a series of numbers, find and replace data or check data for spelling errors. You can also make data stand out in a worksheet by adding borders or changing the font, color, style or alignment of the data.

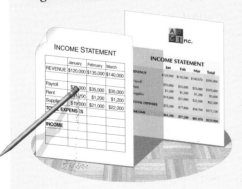

Use Formulas and Functions

Formulas and functions allow you to perform calculations and analyze data in a worksheet. Common calculations include finding the sum, average or total number of values in a list. As you work, Excel checks your formulas for problems and can help you correct common errors in your formulas.

Print Worksheets

You can produce a paper copy of a worksheet you create. Before printing, you can see on your screen how the worksheet will look when printed. Excel also allows you to adjust the margins or change the size of printed data.

Create Charts and Objects

Excel helps you create colorful charts from worksheet data to visually display the data. You can also create objects, such as AutoShapes, WordArt and diagrams, to enhance the appearance of a worksheet and illustrate important concepts.

Manage Data in a List

Excel provides tools that help you manage and analyze a large collection of data, such as a mailing list or product list. You can sort or filter the data in a list. You can also add subtotals to summarize the data.

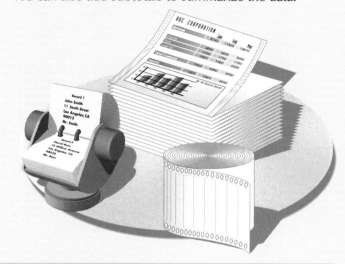

Use Speech Recognition

Speech recognition allows you to use your voice to enter data into a worksheet. You can also use speech recognition to select commands from menus, toolbars and dialog boxes using your voice.

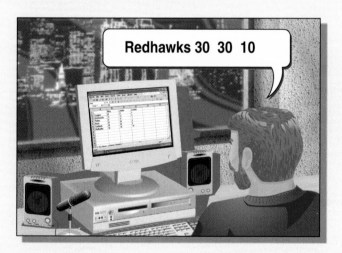

Excel and the Internet

Excel offers features that allow you to take advantage of the Internet. You can create a hyperlink in a workbook to connect the workbook to a Web page. You can also save a workbook you create as a Web page. This allows you to place the workbook on the Internet for other people to view.

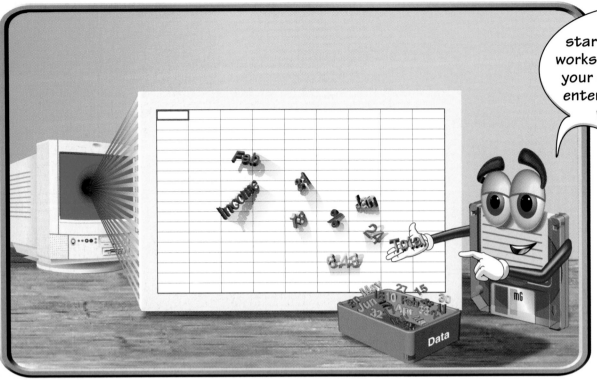

When you start Excel, a blank worksheet appears on your screen. You can enter data into this worksheet.

The New Workbook task pane also appears when you start Excel. You can use the task pane to quickly perform common tasks in Excel.

START EXCEL

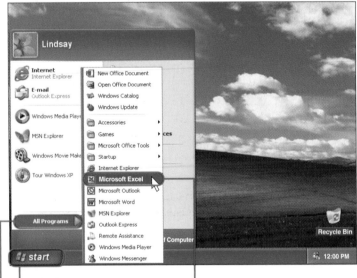

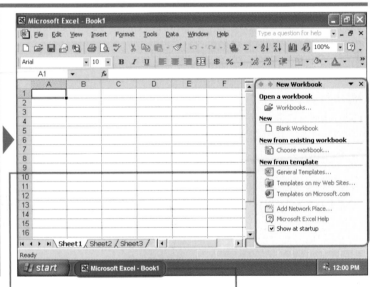

■ Click **start**.

■ Click **All Programs** to view a list of the programs on your computer.

Note: If you are using an earlier version of Windows, click **Programs** in step 2.

■ Click **Microsoft Excel**.

■ The Microsoft Excel window appears, displaying a blank worksheet.

■ This area displays the New Workbook task pane, which allows you to quickly perform common tasks. For information on using the task pane, see page 18.

■ A button for the Microsoft Excel window appears on the taskbar.

6

The Excel window displays many items you can use to work with your data.

Title Bar

Shows the name of the displayed workbook.

Menu Bar

Provides access to lists of commands available in Excel and displays an area where you can type a question to get help information.

Standard Toolbar

Contains buttons you can use to select common commands, such as Save and Print.

Formatting Toolbar

Contains buttons you can use to select common formatting commands, such as Bold and Underline.

Formula Bar

Displays the cell reference and the contents of the active cell. A cell reference identifies the location of each cell in a worksheet and consists of a column letter followed by a row number, such as **A1**.

Active Cell

Displays a thick border. You enter data into the active cell.

Cell

The area where a row and column intersect.

Column

A vertical line of cells. A letter identifies each column.

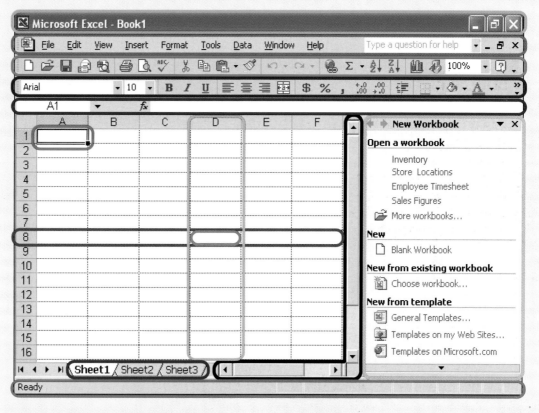

Row

A horizontal line of cells. A number identifies each row.

Status Bar

Displays information about the task you are performing.

Worksheet Tabs

An Excel file is called a workbook. Each workbook is divided into several worksheets. Excel displays a tab for each worksheet.

Scroll Bars

Allow you to browse through a worksheet.

Task Pane

Contains options you can select to perform common tasks, such as opening or creating a workbook.

You can make any cell in your worksheet the active cell. You enter data into the active cell.

You can make only one cell in your worksheet active at a time.

CHANGE THE ACTIVE CELL

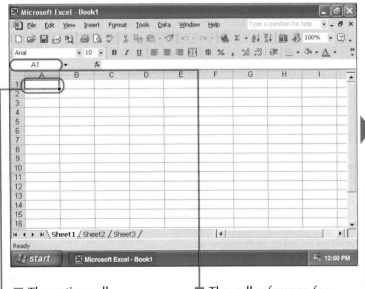

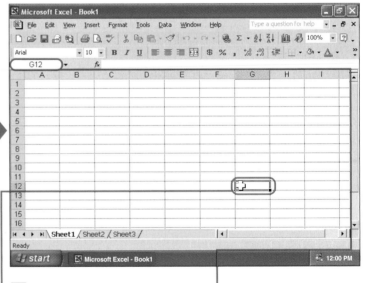

■ The active cell displays a thick border.

■ The cell reference for the active cell appears in this area. A cell reference identifies the location of each cell in a worksheet and consists of a column letter followed by a row number (example: **A1**).

1 Click the cell you want to make the active cell.

Note: You can also press the ←, →, ↑ or ↓ key to change the active cell.

■ The cell reference for the new active cell appears in this area.

You can scroll through your worksheet to view other areas of the worksheet. This is useful when your worksheet contains a lot of data and your computer screen cannot display all the data at once.

SCROLL THROUGH A WORKSHEET

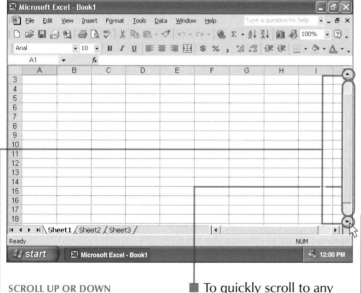

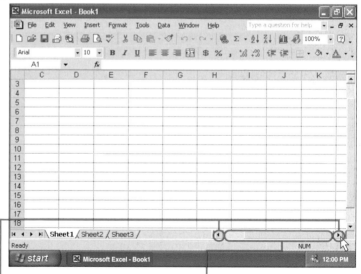

SCROLL UP OR DOWN

1 To scroll up or down one row, click ▲ or ▼.

■ To quickly scroll to any row in your worksheet, position the mouse ⟋ over the scroll box and then drag the scroll box along the scroll bar until the row you want to view appears.

SCROLL LEFT OR RIGHT

1 To scroll left or right one column, click ◄ or ►.

■ To quickly scroll to any column in your worksheet, position the mouse ⟋ over the scroll box and then drag the scroll box along the scroll bar until the column you want to view appears.

SALES REPORT IN UNITS

	1998	1999	2000	2001
January	10500	8850	9000	10400
February	9400	9750	9500	9850
March	6450	8450	8950	9900
April	7890	9000	9400	10850
May	8920	7359	8700	11500

You can enter data into your worksheet quickly and easily.

ENTER DATA

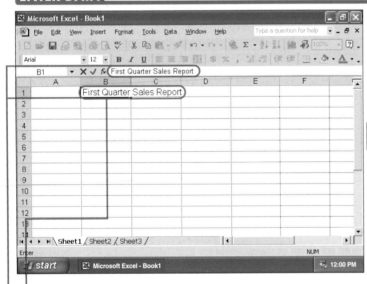

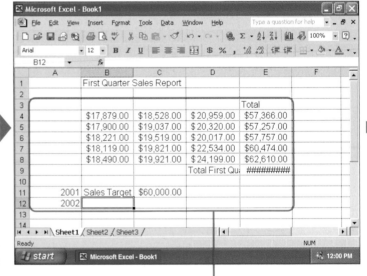

1 Click the cell where you want to enter data. Then type the data.

■ The data you type appears in the active cell and in the formula bar.

■ If you make a typing mistake while entering data, press the ◆Backspace key to remove the incorrect data. Then type the correct data.

2 Press the Enter key to enter the data and move down one cell.

Note: To enter the data and move one cell in any direction, press the ←, →, ↑ or ↓ key.

3 Repeat steps 1 and 2 until you finish entering all your data.

Note: In this book, the size of data was changed to 12 points to make the data easier to read. To change the size of data, see page 91.

10

How can I quickly enter numbers?

You can use the number keys on the right side of your keyboard to quickly enter numbers into your worksheet. To be able to use these number keys, **NUM** must be displayed at the bottom of your screen. You can press the `Num Lock` key to display **NUM** on your screen.

Why did Excel change the appearance of a date I entered?

When you enter a date into your worksheet, Excel may change the format of the date to one of the following date formats: 3/14/2001, 14-Mar or 14-Mar-01. To change the format of dates, see page 104.

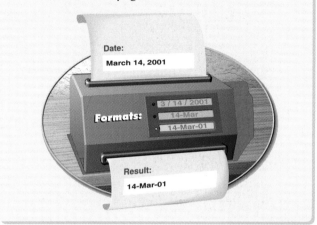

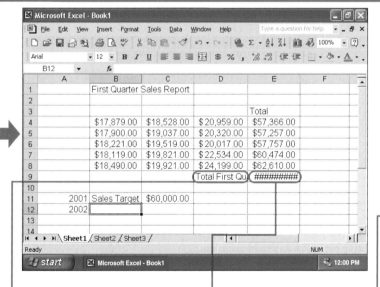

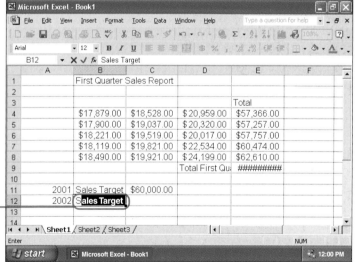

■ If text is too long to fit in a cell, the text will spill into the neighboring cell. If the neighboring cell contains data, Excel will display as much of the text as the column width will allow.

■ If a number is too large to fit in a cell, Excel will display the number in scientific notation or as number signs (#).

Note: To change the width of a column to display text or a number, see page 48.

AUTOCOMPLETE

■ If the first few letters you type match the text in another cell in the same column, Excel will complete the text for you.

1 To enter the text Excel provides, press the `Enter` key.

■ To enter different text, continue typing.

Before performing many tasks in Excel, you must select the cells you want to work with. Selected cells appear highlighted on your screen.

SELECT CELLS

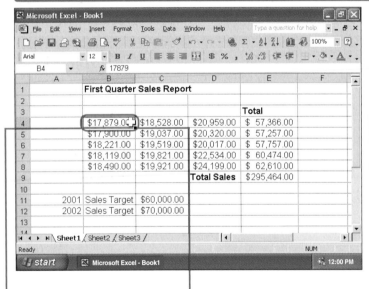

SELECT A CELL

1 Click the cell you want to select.

■ The cell becomes the active cell and displays a thick border.

SELECT A GROUP OF CELLS

1 Position the mouse ⊹ over the first cell you want to select.

2 Drag the mouse ⊹ until you highlight all the cells you want to select.

■ To select multiple groups of cells, press and hold down the **Ctrl** key as you repeat steps **1** and **2** for each group of cells you want to select.

■ To deselect cells, click any cell.

How do I select all the cells in my worksheet?

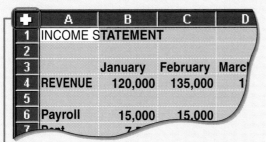

■ To select all the cells in your worksheet, click the box (▭) at the top left corner of your worksheet where the row numbers and column letters meet.

How do I select data in a cell?

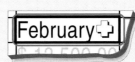

1 To select data in a cell, double-click the cell that contains the data.

2 Drag the mouse I over the data in the cell until you highlight all the data you want to select.

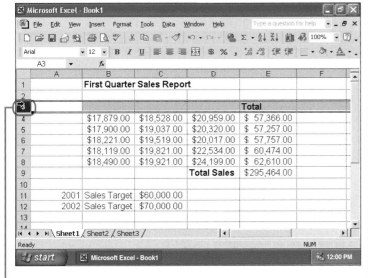

SELECT A ROW

1 Click the number of the row you want to select.

■ To select multiple rows, position the mouse ➡ over the number of the first row you want to select. Then drag the mouse ➡ until you highlight all the rows you want to select.

SELECT A COLUMN

1 Click the letter of the column you want to select.

■ To select multiple columns, position the mouse ⬇ over the letter of the first column you want to select. Then drag the mouse ⬇ until you highlight all the columns you want to select.

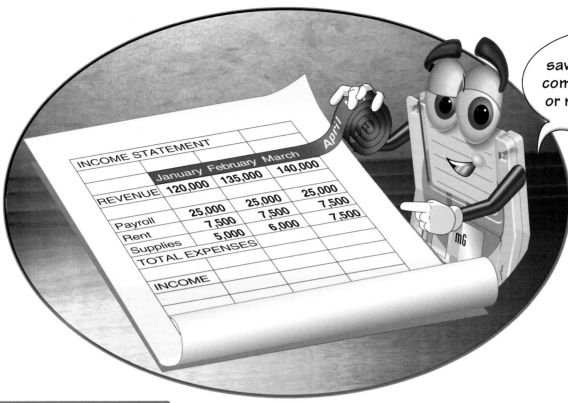

Excel can save you time by completing a text or number series for you.

You can complete a series across a row or down a column in a worksheet. Excel completes a text series based on the text you enter in one cell. Excel completes a number series based on the numbers you enter in two cells.

COMPLETE A TEXT SERIES

1 Enter the text you want to start the series.

2 Click the cell containing the text you entered.

3 Position the mouse ⊕ over the bottom right corner of the cell (⊕ changes to +).

4 Drag the mouse + over the cells you want to include in the series.

■ The cells display the text series.

Note: If Excel cannot determine the text series you want to complete, it will copy the text in the first cell to all the cells you select.

■ To deselect cells, click any cell.

Why does the Auto Fill Options button () appear when I complete a series?

You can use the Auto Fill Options button (📑) to change the way Excel completes a series. For example, you can specify that Excel should not use the formatting from the original cell. Click the Auto Fill Options button to display a list of options and then select the option you want to use. The Auto Fill Options button is available only until you perform another task.

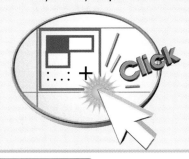

Can I complete a series that will repeat data in several cells?

Yes. Perform steps **1** to **4** on page 15, except enter the same text or data into the first two cells in step **1**. Excel will repeat the information in all the cells you select.

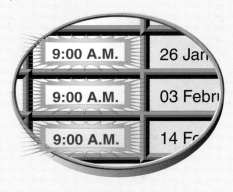

COMPLETE A NUMBER SERIES

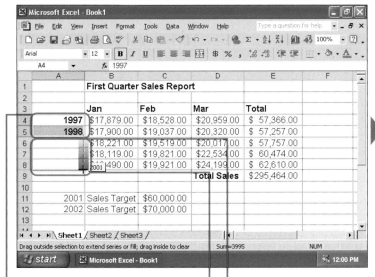

1 Enter the first two numbers you want to start the series.

2 Select the cells containing the numbers you entered. To select cells, see page 12.

3 Position the mouse 🔲 over the bottom right corner of the selected cells (🔲 changes to +).

4 Drag the mouse + over the cells you want to include in the series.

■ The cells display the number series.

■ To deselect cells, click any cell.

You can select a command from a menu or toolbar to perform a task in Excel.

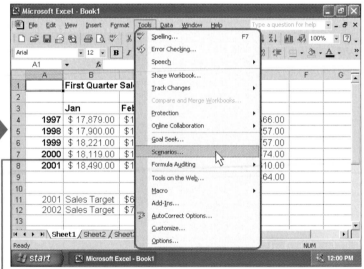

When you first start Excel, the most commonly used commands and buttons appear on each menu and toolbar. As you work, Excel customizes the menus and toolbars to display the commands and buttons you use most often.

SELECT A COMMAND

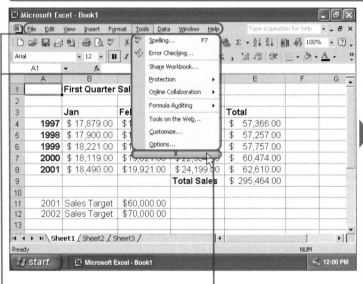

USING MENUS

1 Click the name of the menu you want to display.

■ A short version of the menu appears, displaying the most commonly used commands.

2 To expand the menu and display all the commands, position the mouse ⬚ over ⯗.

Note: If you do not perform step 2, the expanded menu will automatically appear after a few seconds.

■ The expanded menu appears, displaying all the commands.

3 Click the command you want to use.

Note: A dimmed command is currently not available.

■ To close a menu without selecting a command, click outside the menu.

How can I make a command appear on the short version of a menu?

When you select a command from an expanded menu, the command is automatically added to the short version of the menu. The next time you display the short version of the menu, the command you selected will appear.

Expanded Menu

Short Menu

How can I quickly select a command?

You can use a shortcut menu to quickly select a command.

1 Right-click an item you want to change. A shortcut menu appears, displaying the most frequently used commands for the item.

2 Click the command you want to use.

■ To close a shortcut menu without selecting a command, click outside the menu.

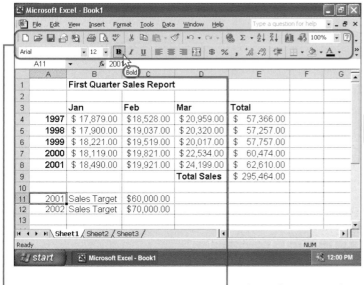

USING TOOLBARS

1 To display the name of a toolbar button, position the mouse ⬚ over the button.

■ After a few seconds, the name of the button appears in a yellow box. The button name can help you determine the task the button performs.

2 A toolbar may not be able to display all of its buttons. Click ⬚ to display additional buttons for the toolbar.

■ Additional buttons for the toolbar appear.

3 To use a toolbar button to select a command, click the button.

USING THE TASK PANE

You can use the task pane to perform common tasks in Excel. The task pane appears each time you start Excel.

You can display or hide the task pane at any time. When you perform some tasks, such as searching for a workbook, the task pane will automatically appear.

USING THE TASK PANE

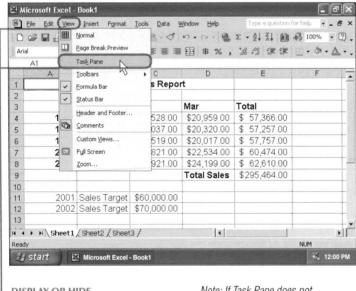

DISPLAY OR HIDE THE TASK PANE

1 Click **View**.

2 Click **Task Pane**.

Note: If Task Pane does not appear on the menu, position the mouse over the bottom of the menu to display all the menu options.

■ The task pane appears or disappears.

■ You can click ▲ or ▼ to browse through the information in the task pane.

■ To quickly hide the task pane at any time, click ⊠.

What task panes are available in Excel?

New Workbook

Allows you to open workbooks and create new workbooks. For information on opening a workbook, see page 30.

Clipboard

Displays each item you have selected to move or copy. For information on moving and copying data, see page 40.

Search

Allows you to search for workbooks on your computer. For information on searching for workbooks, see page 32.

Insert Clip Art

Allows you to add clip art images to your worksheets. For information on adding clip art images, see page 168.

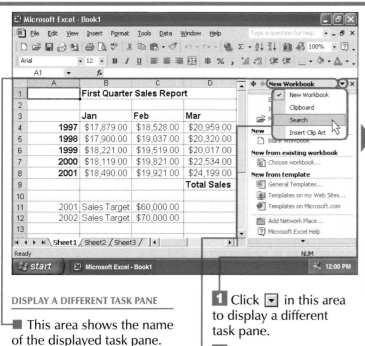

DISPLAY A DIFFERENT TASK PANE

■ This area shows the name of the displayed task pane.

1 Click ▾ in this area to display a different task pane.

2 Click the task pane you want to display.

■ The task pane you selected appears.

■ In this example, the Search task pane appears.

GETTING HELP

If you do not know how to perform a task in Excel, you can ask a question to find help information for the task. Asking a question allows you to quickly find help information of interest.

HELP DESK

GETTING HELP

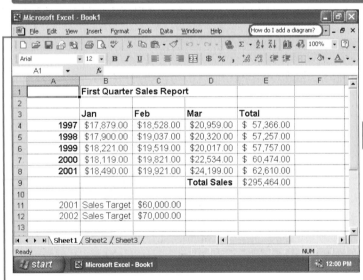

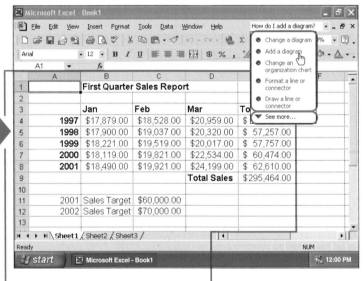

1 Click this area and type your question. Then press the **Enter** key.

■ A list of help topics related to your question appears.

2 Click a help topic of interest.

■ If more help topics exist, you can click **See more** to view the additional topics.

What other ways can I obtain help?

In the Microsoft Excel Help window, you can use the following tabs to obtain help information.

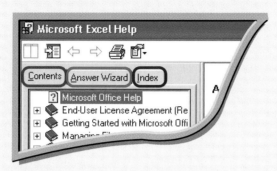

Index

You can type a word of interest or double-click a word in an alphabetical list of help topics. A list of related help topics will appear.

Contents

You can double-click a book icon (📘) or click a page icon (❓) to browse through the contents of Microsoft Excel Help.

Answer Wizard

You can type a question about a topic of interest. A list of help topics related to your question will appear.

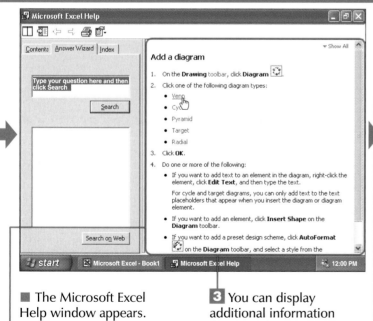

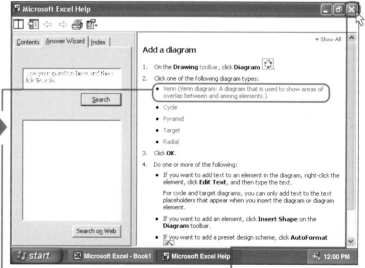

■ The Microsoft Excel Help window appears.

Note: To maximize the Microsoft Excel Help window to fill your screen, click 🔲 in the top right corner of the window.

■ This area displays information about the help topic you selected.

3 You can display additional information for a word or phrase that appears in color. To display the additional information for a colored word or phrase, click the word or phrase.

■ The additional information appears.

Note: The additional information may be a definition, list of steps or tips.

■ To once again hide the additional information, click the colored word or phrase.

4 When you finish reviewing the help information, click ✖ to close the Microsoft Excel Help window.

CHAPTER 2

SAVE AND OPEN YOUR WORKBOOKS

Are you wondering how to save, close or open an Excel workbook? Learn how in this chapter.

SAVE A WORKBOOK

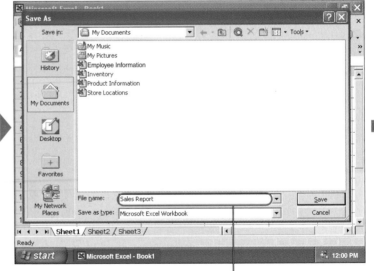

1 Click 🖫 to save your workbook.

Note: If 🖫 is not displayed, click ⯮ on the Standard toolbar to display the button.

■ The Save As dialog box appears.

Note: If you previously saved your workbook, the Save As dialog box will not appear since you have already named the workbook.

2 Type a name for the workbook.

*Note: A workbook name cannot contain the * : ? > < | or " characters.*

What are the commonly used locations that I can access?

History	**My Documents**	**Desktop**	**Favorites**	**My Network Places**
Provides access to folders and workbooks you recently worked with.	Provides a convenient place to store a workbook.	Allows you to store a workbook on the Windows desktop.	Provides a place to store a workbook you will frequently use.	Allows you to store a workbook on your network.

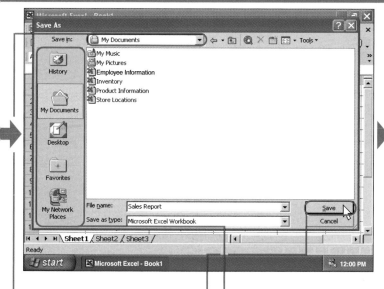

■ This area shows the location where Excel will store your workbook. You can click this area to change the location.

■ This area allows you to access commonly used locations. You can click a location to save your workbook in the location.

3 Click **Save** to save your workbook.

■ Excel saves your workbook and displays the name of the workbook at the top of your screen.

SAVE CHANGES

You should regularly save changes you make to a workbook to avoid losing your work.

1 Click 🔲 to save the changes you made to your workbook.

25

You can create a new workbook to store new data, such as a budget or sales report.

CREATE A NEW WORKBOOK

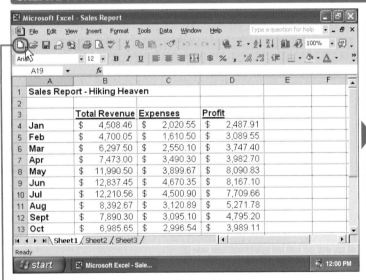

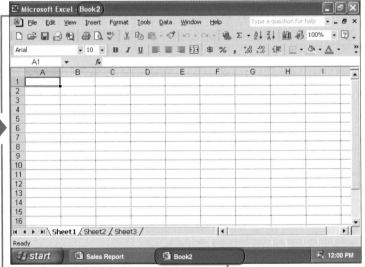

1 Click 🗋 to create a new workbook.

Note: If 🗋 is not displayed, click ⏩ on the Standard toolbar to display the button.

■ A new workbook appears. The previous workbook is now hidden behind the new workbook.

■ Excel gives the new workbook a temporary name, such as Book2, until you save the workbook. To save a workbook, see page 24.

■ A button for the new workbook appears on the taskbar.

SWITCH BETWEEN WORKBOOKS

You can have several workbooks open at once. Excel allows you to easily switch from one open workbook to another.

SWITCH BETWEEN WORKBOOKS

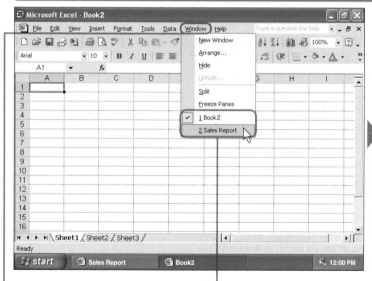

1 Click **Window** to display a list of all the workbooks you have open.

2 Click the name of the workbook you want to switch to.

■ The workbook appears.

■ This area shows the name of the displayed workbook.

■ The taskbar displays a button for each open workbook. You can also click the buttons on the taskbar to switch between the open workbooks.

CLOSE A WORKBOOK

> When you finish working with a workbook, you can close the workbook to remove it from your screen.

When you close a workbook, you do not exit the Excel program. You can continue to work with other workbooks.

CLOSE A WORKBOOK

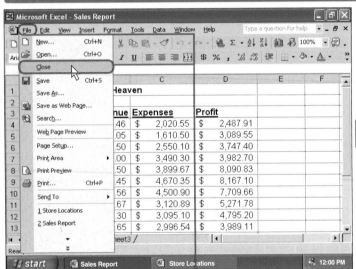

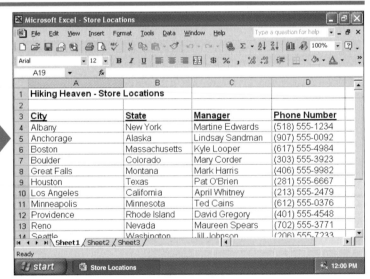

■ Before closing a workbook, you should save any changes you made to the workbook. To save a workbook, see page 24.

1 Click **File**.

2 Click **Close** to close the workbook.

■ The workbook disappears from your screen.

■ If you had more than one workbook open, the second last workbook you worked with appears on your screen.

EXIT EXCEL

When you finish using Excel, you can exit the program.

You should always exit all open programs before turning off your computer.

EXIT EXCEL

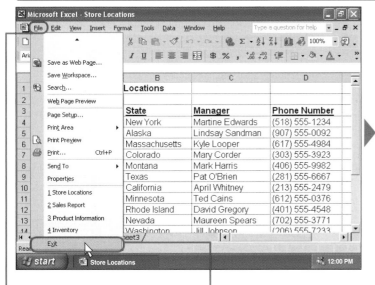

■ Before exiting Excel, you should save all your open workbooks. To save a workbook, see page 24.

1 Click **File**.

2 Click **Exit**.

Note: If Exit does not appear on the menu, position the mouse over the bottom of the menu to display all the menu options.

■ The Microsoft Excel window disappears from your screen.

■ The button for the Microsoft Excel window disappears from the taskbar.

You can open a saved workbook to view the workbook on your screen. Opening a workbook allows you to review and make changes to the workbook.

OPEN A WORKBOOK

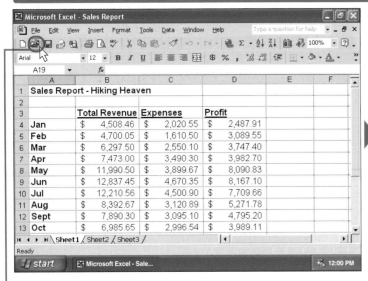

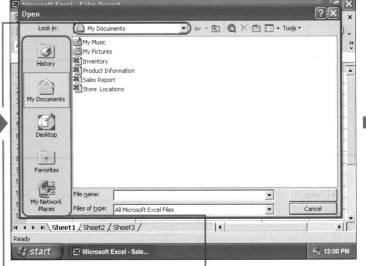

1 Click 📂 to open a workbook.

Note: If 📂 is not displayed, click ⏷ on the Standard toolbar to display the button.

■ The Open dialog box appears.

■ This area shows the location of the displayed workbooks. You can click this area to change the location.

■ This area allows you to access workbooks stored in commonly used locations. You can click a location to display the workbooks stored in the location.

Note: For information on the commonly used locations, see the top of page 25.

30

How can I quickly open a workbook I recently worked with?

Excel remembers the names of the last four workbooks you worked with. You can use one of the following methods to quickly open one of these workbooks.

Use the Task Pane

The New Workbook task pane appears each time you start Excel. To display the New Workbook task pane, see page 18.

1 Click the name of the workbook you want to open.

Use the File Menu

1 Click **File**.

2 Click the name of the workbook you want to open.

Note: If the names of the last four workbooks you worked with are not all displayed, position the mouse ⌖ over the bottom of the menu to display all the names.

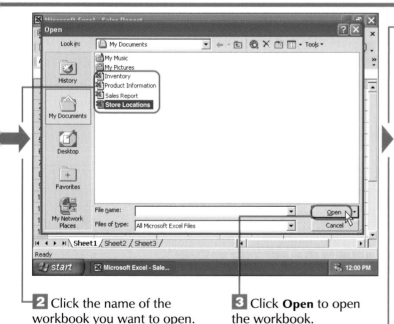

2 Click the name of the workbook you want to open.

3 Click **Open** to open the workbook.

■ The workbook opens and appears on your screen. You can now review and make changes to the workbook.

■ This area displays the name of the workbook.

■ If you already had a workbook open, the new workbook appears in a new Microsoft Excel window. You can click the buttons on the taskbar to switch between the open workbooks.

SEARCH FOR A WORKBOOK

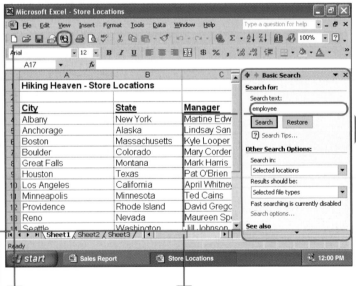

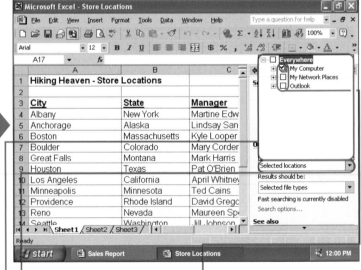

1 Click 🔍 to search for a workbook.

Note: If 🔍 is not displayed, click ⋮ on the Standard toolbar to display the button.

■ The Search task pane appears.

2 Click this area and type one or more words you want to search for.

Note: If this area already contains text, drag the mouse I over the existing text and then perform step 2.

3 Click ▾ in this area to select the locations you want to search.

■ A check mark (✔) appears beside each location that Excel will search.

Note: By default, Excel will search all the drives and folders on your computer.

4 You can click the box beside a location to add (☑) or remove (☐) a check mark.

5 Click outside the list of locations to close the list.

How will Excel use the words I specify to search for workbooks?

Excel will search the contents of workbooks and the file names of workbooks for the words you specify. When searching the contents of workbooks, Excel will search for various forms of the words. For example, searching for "run" will find "run," "running" and "ran."

When selecting the locations and types of files I want to search for, how can I display more items?

Each item that displays a plus sign (⊞) contains hidden items. To display the hidden items, click the plus sign (⊞) beside the item (⊞ changes to ⊟). To once again hide the items, click the minus sign (⊟) beside the item.

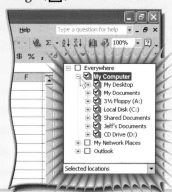

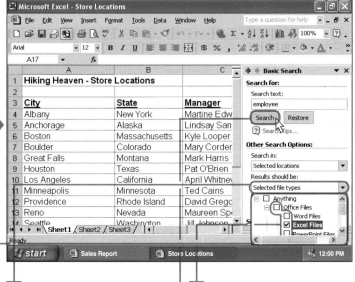

6 Click ▾ in this area to specify the types of files you want to search for.

■ A check mark (✔) appears beside each type of file that Excel will search for.

7 You can click the box beside a file type to add (✔) or remove (☐) a check mark.

8 Click outside the list of file types to close the list.

9 Click **Search** to start the search.

■ This area lists the workbooks that contain the words you specified.

■ To open a workbook in the list, click the workbook.

■ To close the Search task pane at any time, click ✖.

EDIT YOUR WORKSHEETS

Do you want to edit the data in your worksheet or check your worksheet for spelling errors? This chapter teaches you how.

Edit Data 36

Delete Data .38

Undo Changes 39

Move or Copy Data 40

Check Spelling 42

Find Data 44

Replace Data 46

Change Column Width 48

Change Row Height 49

Insert a Row or Column 50

Delete a Row or Column 52

Turn On Smart Tags 54

Using Smart Tags 56

You can edit data in your worksheet to correct a mistake or update data.

EDIT DATA

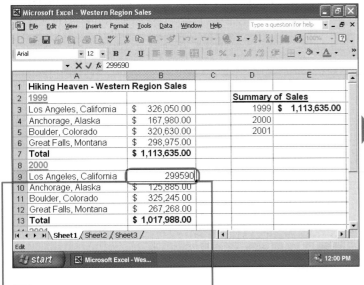

1 Double-click the cell containing the data you want to edit.

■ A flashing insertion point appears in the cell.

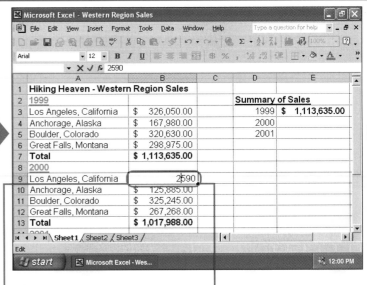

2 Press the ← or → key to move the insertion point to where you want to remove or add characters.

3 To remove the character to the left of the insertion point, press the +Backspace key.

■ To remove the character to the right of the insertion point, press the Delete key.

3 Edit Your Worksheets

EXCEL 2002

Can I edit data in the formula bar?

1 To edit data in the formula bar, click the cell containing the data you want to edit.

■ The formula bar displays the data.

2 Click in the formula bar and then perform steps 2 to 5 below to edit the data.

Can I edit data using only my keyboard?

If you have trouble double-clicking or prefer to use your keyboard, you can use only your keyboard to edit data. Press the ←, →, ↑ or ↓ key to select the cell you want to make the active cell and then press the F2 key to edit the data in the active cell. The insertion point appears at the end of the data in the cell.

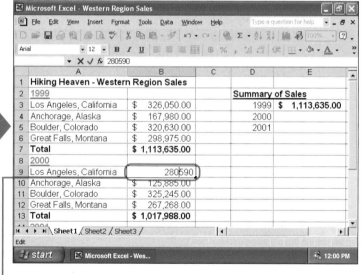

4 To add data where the insertion point flashes on your screen, type the data.

5 When you finish making changes to the data, press the Enter key.

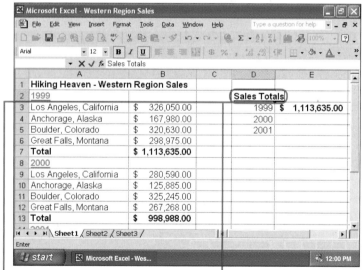

REPLACE ALL DATA IN A CELL

1 Click the cell containing the data you want to replace with new data.

2 Type the new data and then press the Enter key.

37

You can remove data you no longer need from cells in your worksheet. You can delete data from a single cell or from several cells at once.

When you delete the data in a cell, Excel does not remove the formatting you applied to the cell, such as a new font or color. Any new data you enter into the cell will display the same formatting as the data you deleted. To clear the formatting from cells, see page 107.

DELETE DATA

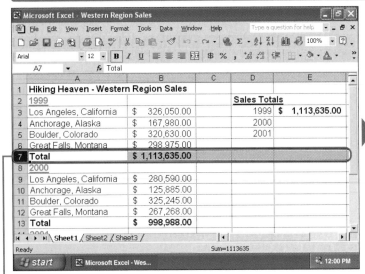

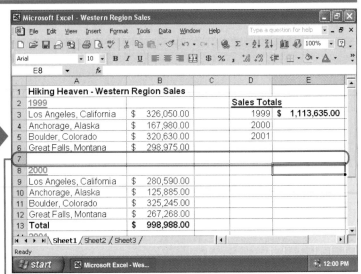

1 Select the cells containing the data you want to delete. To select cells, see page 12.

2 Press the Delete key.

■ The data in the cells you selected disappears.

■ To deselect cells, click any cell.

UNDO CHANGES

Excel remembers the last changes you made to your worksheet. If you regret these changes, you can cancel them by using the Undo feature.

The Undo feature can cancel your last editing and formatting changes.

UNDO CHANGES

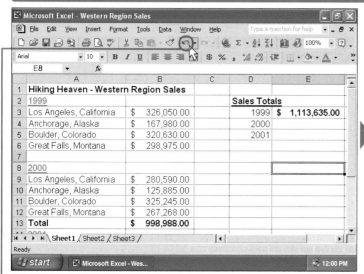

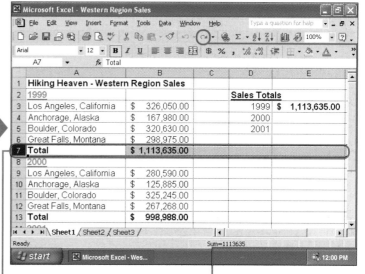

1 Click ⤺ to undo the last change you made to your worksheet.

Note: If ⤺ is not displayed, click ⟫ on the Standard toolbar to display the button.

■ Excel cancels the last change you made to your worksheet.

■ You can repeat step **1** to cancel previous changes you made.

■ To reverse the results of using the Undo feature, click ⤼.

Note: If ⤼ is not displayed, click ⟫ on the Standard toolbar to display the button.

39

You can move or copy data to a new location in your worksheet.

Moving data allows you to reorganize data in your worksheet. When you move data, the data disappears from its original location.

Copying data allows you to repeat data in your worksheet without having to retype the data. When you copy data, the data appears in both the original and new locations.

MOVE OR COPY DATA

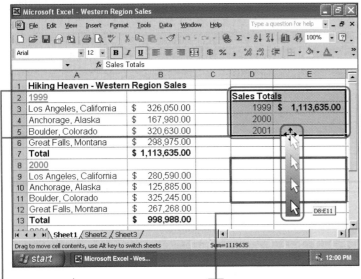

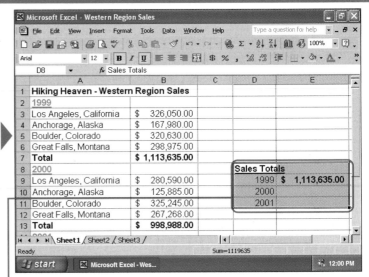

USING DRAG AND DROP

1 Select the cells containing the data you want to move. To select cells, see page 12.

2 Position the mouse ⊕ over a border of the selected cells (⊕ changes to ✛).

3 To move the data, drag the mouse ↖ to where you want to place the data.

Note: A gray box indicates where the data will appear.

■ The data moves to the new location.

■ To copy data, perform steps 1 to 3, except press and hold down the Ctrl key as you perform step 3.

40

How can I use the Clipboard task pane to move or copy data?

The Clipboard task pane displays up to the last 24 items you have selected to move or copy using the toolbar buttons. To place a clipboard item into your worksheet, click the cell where you want to place the item and then click the item in the task pane. For more information on the task pane, see page 18.

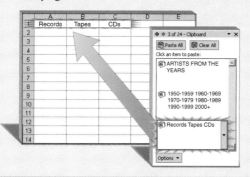

Why does the Paste Options button (📋) appear when I copy data?

You can use the Paste Options button (📋) to change the way Excel copies data when you use the Copy button (📋). For example, you can specify that you want to use the column width from the original cells in the new location. Click the Paste Options button to display a list of options and then select the option you want to use. The Paste Options button is available only until you perform another task.

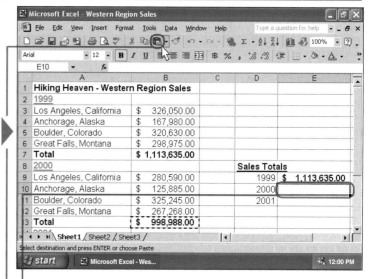

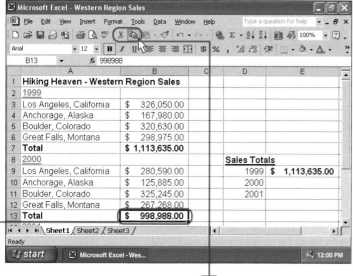

USING THE TOOLBAR BUTTONS

1 Select the cells containing the data you want to move or copy. To select cells, see page 12.

2 Click one of the following buttons.

- ✂ Move data
- 📋 Copy data

Note: The Clipboard task pane may appear, displaying items you have selected to move or copy. To use the Clipboard task pane, see the top of this page.

3 Click the cell where you want to place the data. This cell will become the top left cell of the new location.

4 Click 📋 to place the data in the new location.

Note: If 📋 is not displayed, click 📄 on the Standard toolbar to display the button.

■ The data appears in the new location.

You can find and correct all the spelling errors in your worksheet.

Spelling Error: wether

Suggestions: weather wetter whether wither

Excel compares every word in your worksheet to words in its dictionary. If a word in your worksheet does not exist in the dictionary, the word is considered misspelled.

CHECK SPELLING

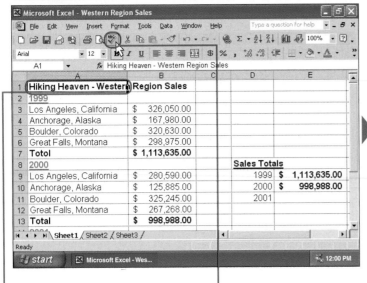

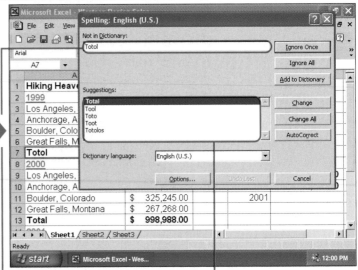

1 Click cell **A1** to start the spell check at the beginning of your worksheet.

2 Click 🔤 to start the spell check.

Note: If 🔤 is not displayed, click ⋙ on the Standard toolbar to display the button.

■ The Spelling dialog box appears if Excel finds a misspelled word.

■ This area displays the misspelled word.

■ This area displays suggestions for correcting the word.

What parts of a worksheet does Excel check for spelling errors?

In addition to text in cells, Excel spell checks text in items such as charts, AutoShapes, text boxes, diagrams and headers and footers.

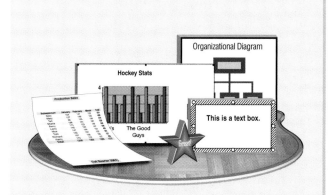

Can Excel automatically correct my typing mistakes?

Yes. Excel automatically corrects common spelling errors as you type. Here are a few examples.

adn	⟹	and
alot	⟹	a lot
comittee	⟹	committee
don;t	⟹	don't
nwe	⟹	new
occurence	⟹	occurrence
recieve	⟹	receive
seperate	⟹	separate
teh	⟹	the

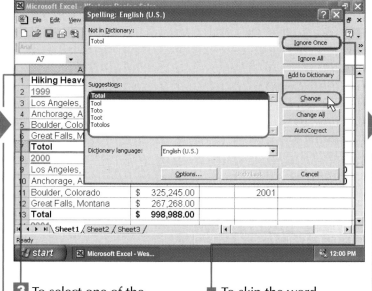

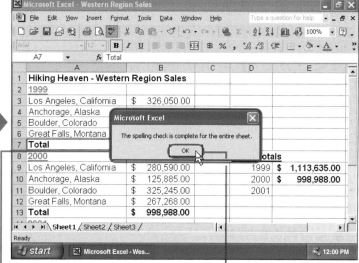

3 To select one of the suggestions, click the suggestion.

4 Click **Change** to correct the word in your worksheet.

■ To skip the word and continue checking your worksheet, click **Ignore Once**.

*Note: To skip the word and all occurrences of the word in your worksheet, click **Ignore All**.*

5 Correct or ignore misspelled words until this dialog box appears, telling you the spell check is complete.

6 Click **OK** to close the dialog box.

FIND DATA

You can use the Find feature to quickly locate every occurrence of a word or number in your worksheet.

FIND DATA

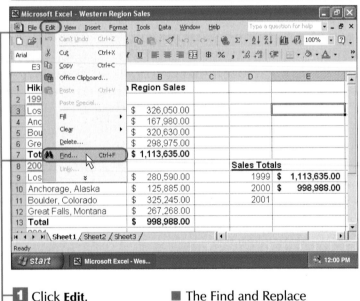

1 Click **Edit**.

2 Click **Find**.

■ The Find and Replace dialog box appears.

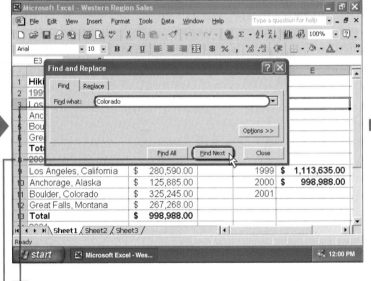

3 Type the word or number you want to find.

4 Click **Find Next** to start the search.

*Note: A dialog box appears if Excel cannot find the word or number you specified. Click **OK** to close the dialog box and then skip to step **6**.*

Can I search for part of a word or number?

When you search for data in your worksheet, Excel will find the data you specify even when the data is part of a larger word or number. For example, if you search for the number 105, Excel will also find the numbers **105**.35, 2**105** and **105**6.

Can I search only a specific section of my worksheet?

Yes. To search only a specific section of your worksheet, select the cells you want to search before starting the search. To select cells, see page 12.

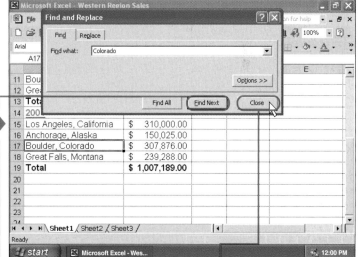

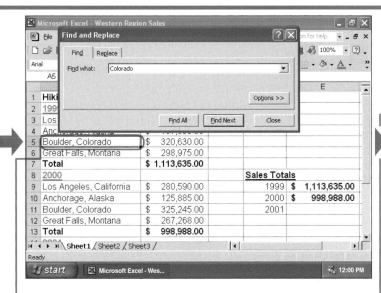

■ Excel highlights the first cell containing the word or number.

Note: If the Find and Replace dialog box covers a cell containing the word or number you want to find, Excel will automatically move the dialog box to a new location.

5 Click **Find Next** to find the next matching word or number. Repeat this step until you find the word or number you are searching for.

6 To close the Find and Replace dialog box at any time, click **Close**.

You can find and replace every occurrence of a word or number in your worksheet. This is useful if you have incorrectly entered data throughout your worksheet.

REPLACE DATA

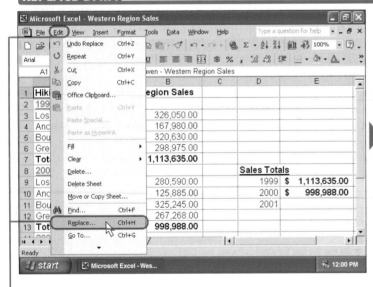

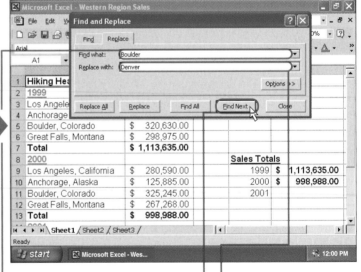

1 Click **Edit**.

2 Click **Replace**.

Note: If Replace does not appear on the menu, position the mouse over the bottom of the menu to display all the menu options.

■ The Find and Replace dialog box appears.

3 Type the word or number you want to replace with new data.

4 Click this area and type the word or number you want to replace the data you typed in step 3.

Note: If these areas already contain data, drag the mouse I over the existing data and then type the word or number.

5 Click **Find Next** to start the search.

Can Excel find and replace a number used in my formulas?

Yes. Excel automatically searches the formulas in your worksheet for the number you specified. This is useful if you want to change a number used in several formulas. For example, if sales tax increases from 7% to 8%, you can search for all occurrences of **.07** in your formulas and replace them with **.08**.

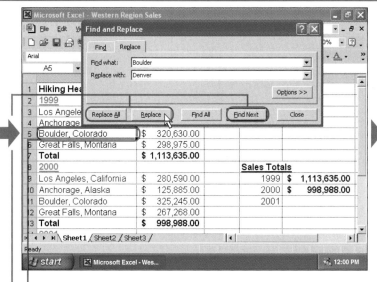

Can I use wildcard characters to find the data I want to replace?

Yes. You can use an asterisk (*) or a question mark (?) to find the data you want to replace. The asterisk (*) represents one or more characters. The question mark (?) represents a single character. For example, type **Wend?** to find Wendi and Wendy.

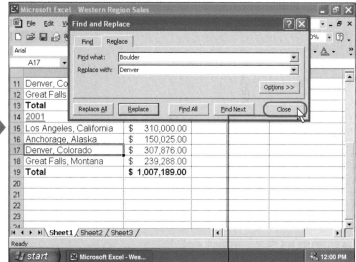

■ Excel highlights the first cell containing the word or number you specified.

6 Click one of these options.

Replace All - Replace all occurrences of the word or number in the worksheet.

Replace - Replace the word or number.

Find Next - Ignore the word or number.

Note: To cancel the search at any time, press the **Esc** *key.*

■ In this example, Excel replaces the word or number and searches for the next match.

7 Replace or ignore matching words or numbers until you find all the occurrences of the word or number you want to replace.

8 Click **Close** to close the Find and Replace dialog box.

CHANGE COLUMN WIDTH

You can improve the appearance of your worksheet by changing the width of columns.

Data in a cell may be hidden if the cell is not wide enough to display the data and the neighboring cell also contains data. You can increase the column width to display all the data in the cell.

CHANGE COLUMN WIDTH

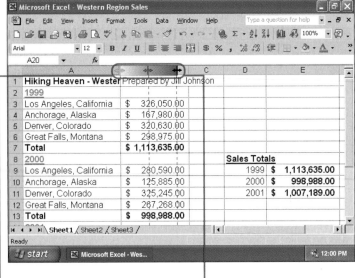

1 To change the width of a column, position the mouse ⬄ over the right edge of the column heading (⬄ changes to ↔).

2 Drag the column edge until the dotted line displays the column width you want.

■ The column displays the new width.

FIT LONGEST ITEM

1 To quickly change a column width to fit the longest item in the column, double-click the right edge of the column heading.

You can change the height of rows to add space between the rows of data in your worksheet.

CHANGE ROW HEIGHT

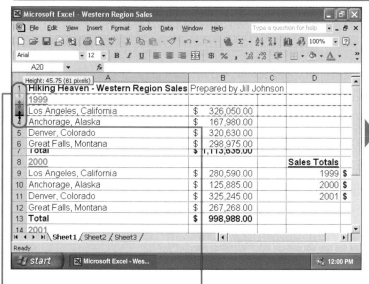

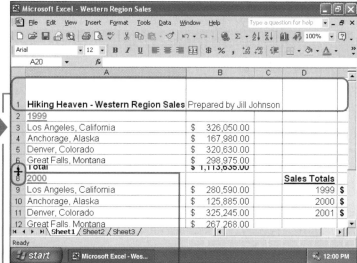

1 To change the height of a row, position the mouse 🔲 over the bottom edge of the row heading (🔲 changes to ➕).

2 Drag the row edge until the dotted line displays the row height you want.

■ The row displays the new height.

FIT TALLEST ITEM

1 To quickly change a row height to fit the tallest item in the row, double-click the bottom edge of the row heading.

49

INSERT A ROW

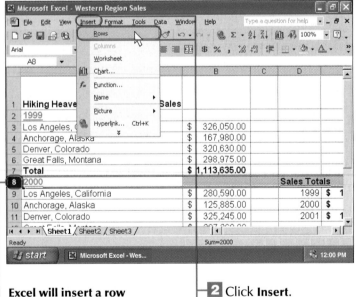

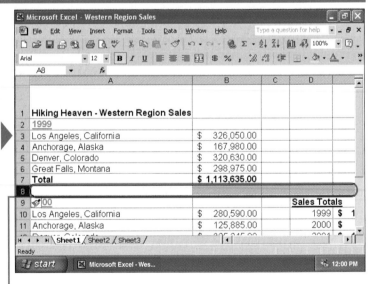

Excel will insert a row above the row you select.

1 To select a row, click the row number.

2 Click **Insert**.

3 Click **Rows**.

■ The new row appears and all the rows that follow shift downward.

■ To deselect a row, click any cell.

Do I need to adjust my formulas when I insert a row or column?

No. When you insert a row or column, Excel automatically updates any formulas affected by the insertion. For information on formulas, see pages 60 to 63.

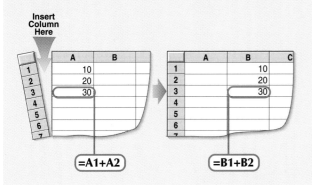

How do I insert several rows or columns at once?

You can use one of the methods shown below to insert several rows or columns at once, but you must first select the number of rows or columns you want to insert. For example, to insert two columns, select two columns and then perform steps **2** and **3** below. To select multiple rows or columns, see page 13.

INSERT A COLUMN

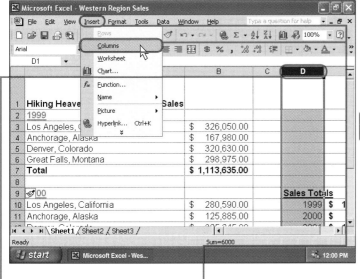

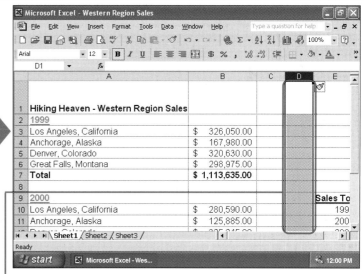

Excel will insert a column to the left of the column you select.

1 To select a column, click the column letter.

2 Click **Insert**.

3 Click **Columns**.

■ The new column appears and all the columns that follow shift to the right.

■ To deselect a column, click any cell.

DELETE A ROW OR COLUMN

You can delete a row or column to remove data you no longer want to display in your worksheet.

DELETE A ROW

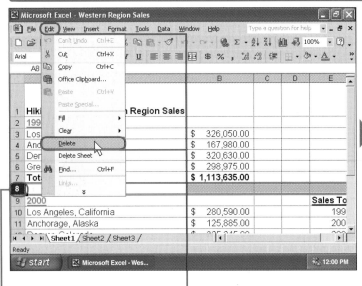

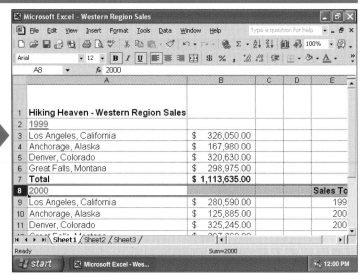

1 To select the row you want to delete, click the row number.

2 Click **Edit**.

3 Click **Delete** to delete the row.

■ The row disappears and all the rows that follow shift upward.

■ To deselect a row, click any cell.

Why did #REF! appear in a cell after I deleted a row or column?

If #REF! appears in a cell in your worksheet, you may have deleted data needed to calculate a formula. Before you delete a row or column, make sure the row or column does not contain data that is used in a formula. For information on formulas, see pages 60 to 63.

How do I delete several rows or columns at once?

You can use one of the methods shown below to delete several rows or columns at once, but you must first select the rows or columns you want to delete. For example, to delete three columns, select the columns and then perform steps 2 and 3 below. To select multiple rows or columns, see page 13.

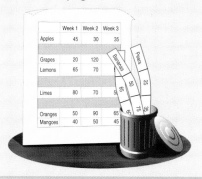

DELETE A COLUMN

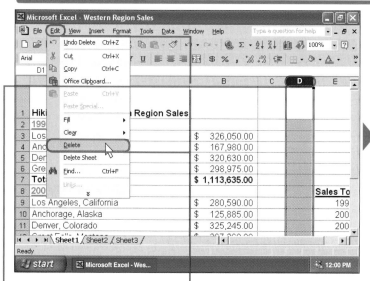

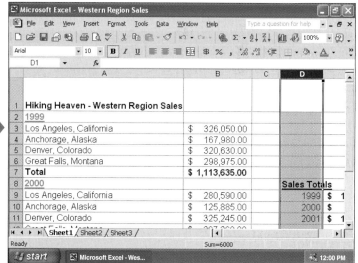

1 To select the column you want to delete, click the column letter.

2 Click **Edit**.

3 Click **Delete** to delete the column.

■ The column disappears and all the columns that follow shift to the left.

■ To deselect a column, click any cell.

You can use smart tags to perform actions in Excel that you would normally have to open another program to perform, such as displaying stock information. Before you can use smart tags in Excel, you must turn on smart tags.

After you turn on smart tags, smart tags will be available in all your workbooks.

TURN ON SMART TAGS

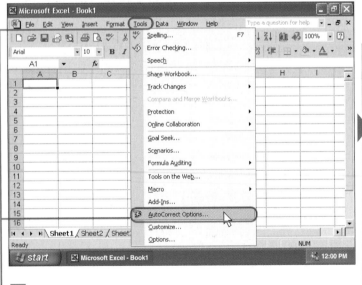

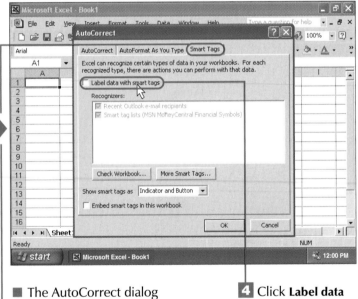

1 Click **Tools**.

2 Click **AutoCorrect Options**.

Note: If AutoCorrect Options does not appear on the menu, position the mouse ₖ over the bottom of the menu to display all the menu options.

■ The AutoCorrect dialog box appears.

3 Click the **Smart Tags** tab.

4 Click **Label data with smart tags** (☐ changes to ✔).

SIMPLIFY IT

What types of data can Excel label with a smart tag?

Recent Outlook e-mail recipients

Excel can label e-mail addresses of people you recently sent messages to using Microsoft Outlook.

Note: After sending an e-mail message to a person using Microsoft Outlook, you may have to restart Outlook and Excel to have Excel label the address with a smart tag.

ddress	Email
59 Beach St.	padams@abccorp.com
00 Pine St.	banderson@abccorp.com
0 Westside St.	mcorder@xyzcorp.com
Mill St.	rmengle@xyzcorp.com
7 North River Rd.	pobrien@abccorp.com

Smart tag lists (MSN MoneyCentral Financial Symbols)

Excel can label financial symbols you type in capital letters with a smart tag. Here are some examples of financial symbols Excel can label with a smart tag.

To obtain information about:	Type:
Microsoft Corporation	MSFT
IBM	IBM
Intel Corporation	INTC
Coca-Cola Bottling Co.	COKE
Pepsi Bottling Group, Inc.	PBG
Hershey Foods Corporation	HSY
NIKE, Inc.	NKE
Reebok International Ltd.	RBK
Columbia Sportswear Company	COLM

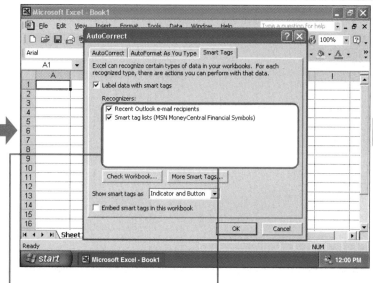

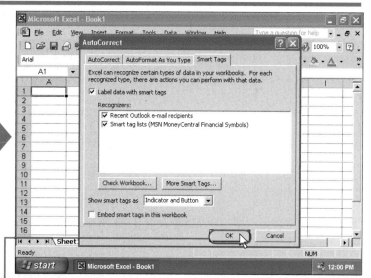

■ This area displays the types of data Excel can label with a smart tag. A check mark (✔) beside a type of data indicates Excel will label the data with a smart tag.

■ You can click the box beside a type of data to add (✔) or remove (☐) a check mark.

5 Click **OK** to confirm your changes.

■ You can now use smart tags in your workbooks.

■ To turn off smart tags for your workbooks, repeat steps 1 to 5, ✔ changes to ☐ in step 4.

Note: You must close and reopen your open workbooks for the change to take effect in the workbooks. To close a workbook, see page 28. To open a workbook, see page 30.

Excel labels certain types of data, such as financial symbols, with smart tags. You can use a smart tag to perform an action, such as getting a stock price or displaying information about a company.

USING SMART TAGS

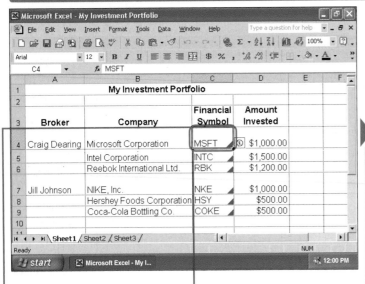

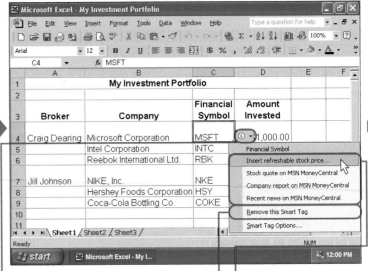

■ A purple triangle appears in the bottom right corner of a cell containing data Excel labels with a smart tag.

1 To perform an action using a smart tag, click a cell containing a purple triangle.

■ The Smart Tag Actions button appears.

2 Click the Smart Tag Actions button to display a list of actions you can perform using the smart tag.

3 Click the action you want to perform.

■ In this example, we insert a refreshable stock price.

■ To remove a smart tag from a cell, click **Remove this Smart Tag**.

How can I refresh a stock price?

To obtain the most up-to-date information for a stock price, click a blank space in the stock price area and then click 🔳 on the External Data toolbar. A spinning icon (🌐) appears on the status bar at the bottom of your screen while the stock price is being refreshed.

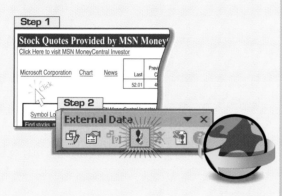

What actions can I perform for an e-mail address labeled with a smart tag?

You can perform one of several actions such as sending the person an e-mail message, scheduling a meeting with the person or adding the person to your list of contacts in Microsoft Outlook.

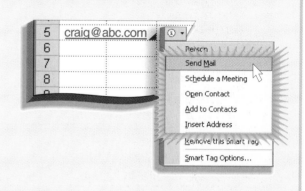

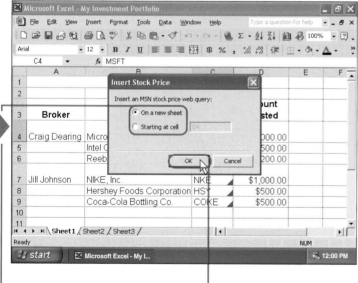

■ The Insert Stock Price dialog box appears.

◀4 Click an option to specify where you want the stock price to appear (○ changes to ⊙).

Note: The stock price may take up a large area of your worksheet.

◀5 Click **OK** to insert the stock price.

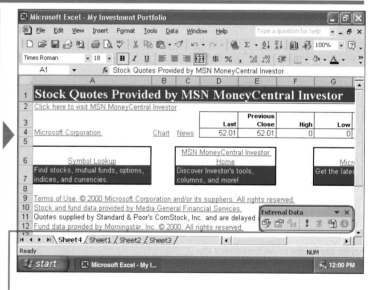

■ In this example, the stock price appears on a new worksheet.

■ The External Data toolbar also appears, displaying buttons you can use to work with the stock price.

Note: To delete a stock price displayed on a worksheet, you can delete the worksheet. To delete a worksheet, see page 137.

CHAPTER 4

WORK WITH FORMULAS AND FUNCTIONS

Would you like to perform calculations on the data in your worksheet? Learn how in this chapter.

A formula allows you to calculate and analyze data in your worksheet.

$= A1 + A2 + A3$

A formula always begins with an equal sign (=).

OPERATORS

A formula can contain one or more operators. An operator specifies the type of calculation you want to perform.

Arithmetic Operators

You can use arithmetic operators to perform mathematical calculations.

	A	B
1	5	5
2		
3	10	

=A1+B1

Operator	Description
+	Addition (A1+B1)
-	Subtraction (A1-B1)
*	Multiplication (A1*B1)
/	Division (A1/B1)
%	Percent (A1%)
^	Exponentiation (A1 ^ B1)

Comparison Operators

You can use comparison operators to compare two values. A formula that uses only a comparison operator will return a value of TRUE or FALSE.

	A	B
1	5	5
2		
3	TRUE	

=A1=B1

Operator	Description
=	Equal to (A1=B1)
>	Greater than (A1>B1)
<	Less than (A1<B1)
>=	Greater than or equal to (A1>=B1)
<=	Less than or equal to (A1<=B1)
<>	Not equal to (A1<>B1)

ORDER OF CALCULATIONS

1	Percent (%)
2	Exponentiation (^)
3	Multiplication (*) and Division (/)
4	Addition (+) and Subtraction (-)
5	Comparison operators

	A
1	2
2	4
3	6
4	8
5	
6	
7	

=A1+A2+A3*A4
=2+4+6*8=54

=A1+(A2+A3)*A4
=2+(4+6)*8=82

=A1*(A3-A2)+A4
=2*(6-4)+8=12

=A2^A1+A3
=4^2+6=22

When a formula contains more than one operator, Excel performs the calculations in a specific order.

You can use parentheses ( ) to change the order in which Excel performs calculations. Excel will perform the calculations inside the parentheses first.

CELL REFERENCES

When entering formulas, use cell references instead of actual data whenever possible. For example, enter the formula =A1+A2 instead of =10+20.

When you use cell references and you change a number used in a formula, Excel will automatically redo the calculation for you.

	A	B
1	10	
2	20	
3		

=A1+A2=30

FUNCTIONS

A function is a ready-to-use formula that you can use to perform a calculation on the data in your worksheet. Examples of commonly used functions include AVERAGE, COUNT, MAX and SUM.

■ A function always begins with an equal sign (=).

■ The data Excel will use to calculate a function is enclosed in parentheses ( ).

	A
1	10
2	20
3	30
4	40
5	
6	

=AVERAGE(A1:A4)
=(10+20+30+40)/4 = 25

=COUNT(A1:A4) = 4

=MAX(A1:A4) = 40

=SUM(A1:A4)
=10+20+30+40 = 100

Specify Individual Cells

When a comma (,) separates cell references in a function, Excel uses each cell to perform the calculation. For example, =SUM(A1,A2,A3) is the same as the formula =A1+A2+A3.

Specify a Group of Cells

When a colon (:) separates cell references in a function, Excel uses the specified cells and all cells between them to perform the calculation.

For example, =SUM(A1:A3) is the same as the formula =A1+A2+A3.

You can enter a formula into any cell in your worksheet. A formula helps you calculate and analyze data in your worksheet.

= B1+B2+B3+B4

EXPENSES

	A	B
1	Rent	
2	Car	$750
3	Insurance	$300
4	Gas	$125
Total		$50
		$1,225

When entering formulas, you should use cell references instead of actual data whenever possible.

A formula always begins with an equal sign (=).

ENTER A FORMULA

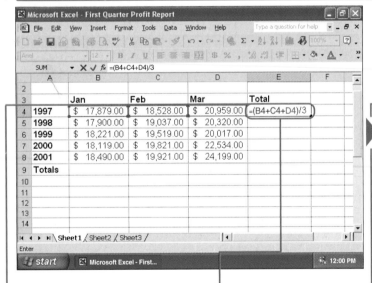

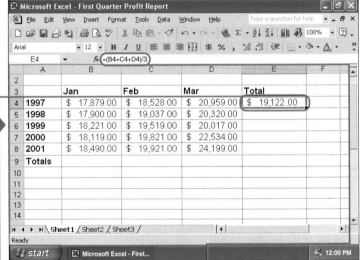

1 Click the cell where you want to enter a formula.

2 Type an equal sign (=) to begin the formula.

3 Type the formula and then press the Enter key.

■ The result of the calculation appears in the cell.

4 To view the formula you entered, click the cell containing the formula.

■ The formula bar displays the formula for the cell.

62

What happens if I change a number used in a formula?

When you use cell references and you change a number used in a formula, Excel will automatically redo the calculation for you.

	A	B
1	Rent	750
2	Car	300
3	Insurance	125
4	Gas	*100* ~~50~~
5	Total	*1,275* ~~1,225~~

1275

How can I quickly enter cell references into a formula?

To quickly enter cell references into a formula, perform steps 1 to 3 on page 62, except click each cell you want to use instead of typing the cell references. This method of entering cell references can help you minimize typing errors.

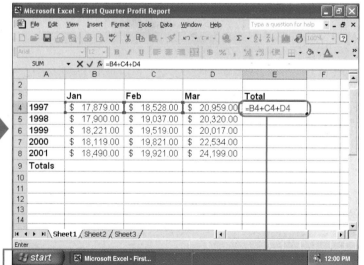

	A	B
1	$2,000.00	
2	$2,500.00	
3	$2,225.00	
4	$2,350.00	
5	= A1+ A2	

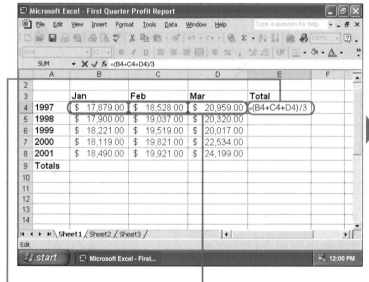

EDIT A FORMULA

1 Double-click the cell containing the formula you want to change.

■ The formula appears in the cell.

■ Excel outlines each cell used in the formula with a different color.

2 Press the ← or → key to move the flashing insertion point to where you want to remove or add characters.

3 To remove the character to the left of the insertion point, press the ◆Backspace key.

■ To add data where the insertion point flashes on your screen, type the data.

4 When you finish making changes to the formula, press the Enter key.

ENTER A FUNCTION

Excel helps you enter functions into your worksheet. Functions allow you to perform calculations without typing long, complex formulas.

=SUM(A1:A4)

=AVERAGE(A1:A4)

=ROUND(E4,2)

=COUNT(B1:B6)

=MAX(E1:E4)

Excel offers over 200 functions to help you analyze data in your worksheet. There are financial functions, math and trigonometry functions, date and time functions, statistical functions and many more.

ENTER A FUNCTION

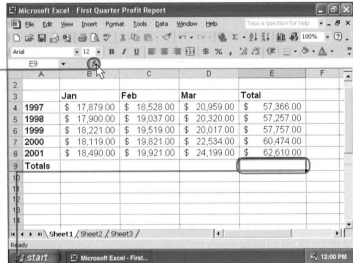

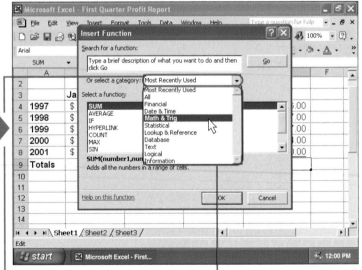

1 Click the cell where you want to enter a function.

2 Click [fx] to enter a function.

■ The Insert Function dialog box appears.

*Note: The Office Assistant may also appear. Click **No** to remove the Office Assistant from your screen.*

3 Click this area to display the categories of available functions.

4 Click the category containing the function you want to use.

*Note: If you do not know which category contains the function you want to use, click **All** to display a list of all the functions.*

Can Excel help me find the function I should use to perform a calculation?

If you do not know which function to use to perform a calculation, you can have Excel recommend a function.

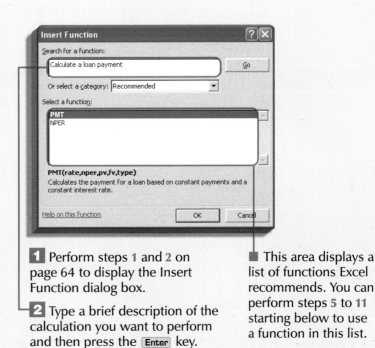

■ **1** Perform steps 1 and 2 on page 64 to display the Insert Function dialog box.

■ **2** Type a brief description of the calculation you want to perform and then press the Enter key.

■ This area displays a list of functions Excel recommends. You can perform steps 5 to 11 starting below to use a function in this list.

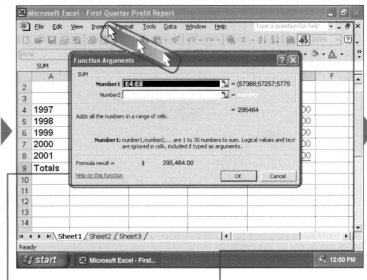

■ This area displays the functions in the category you selected.

■ **5** Click the function you want to use.

■ This area describes the function you selected.

■ **6** Click **OK** to continue.

■ The Function Arguments dialog box appears. If the dialog box covers data you want to use in the calculation, you can move the dialog box to a new location.

■ **7** To move the dialog box, position the mouse over the title bar and then drag the dialog box to a new location.

CONTINUED

When entering a function, you must specify which numbers you want to use in the calculation.

ENTER A FUNCTION (CONTINUED)

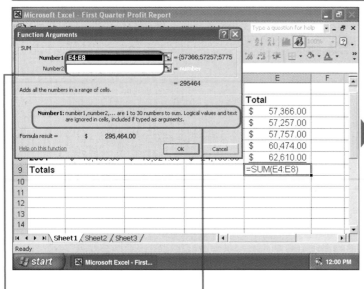

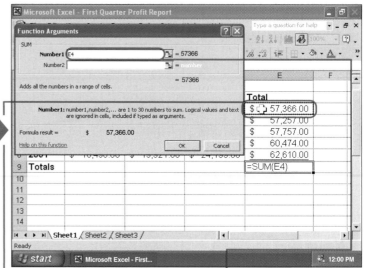

■ This area displays boxes where you enter the numbers you want to use in the calculation.

■ This area describes the numbers you need to enter.

8 To enter the first number for the function, click the cell that contains the number.

Note: If the number you want to use does not appear in your worksheet, type the number.

■ The cell reference for the number appears in this area.

Can I enter a function myself?

If you know the name of the function you want to use, you can type the function and cell references directly into a cell in your worksheet. You must start the function with an equal sign (=), enclose the cell references in parentheses ( ) and separate the cell references with commas (,) or a colon (:).

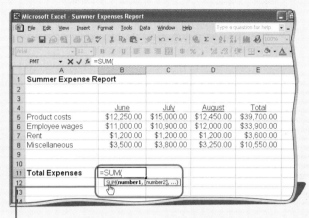

■ When you type a function directly into a cell, a yellow box appears, displaying the name of the function. You can click the name of the function to display help information about the function.

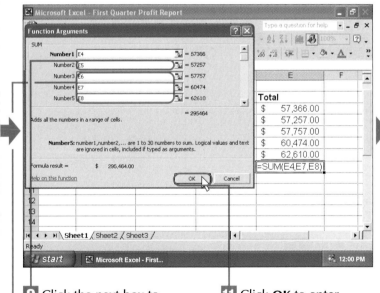

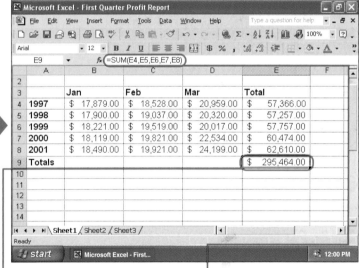

9 Click the next box to enter the next number.

10 Repeat steps **8** and **9** until you have entered all the numbers you want to use in the calculation.

11 Click **OK** to enter the function into your worksheet.

■ The result of the function appears in the cell.

■ The formula bar displays the function for the cell.

You can quickly perform common calculations on numbers in your worksheet. For example, you can calculate the sum of a list of numbers.

PERFORM COMMON CALCULATIONS

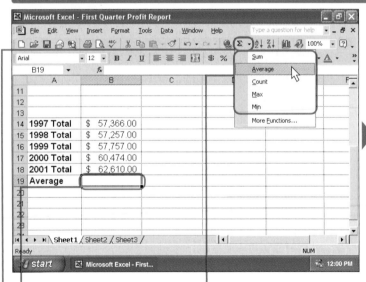

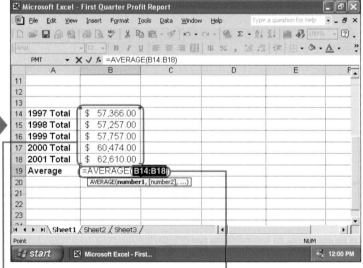

1 Click the cell below or to the right of the cells containing the numbers you want to include in the calculation.

2 Click ⏷ in this area to display a list of common calculations.

Note: If Σ ⏷ is not displayed, click » on the Standard toolbar to display the button.

3 Click the calculation you want to perform.

Note: If you want to quickly add the numbers, you can click Σ instead of performing steps 2 and 3.

■ A moving outline appears around the cells that Excel will include in the calculation.

■ If Excel outlines the wrong cells, you can select the cells that contain the numbers you want to include in the calculation. To select cells, see page 12.

■ The cell you selected in step 1 displays the function Excel will use to perform the calculation.

What common calculations can I perform?

Sum	Adds a list of numbers.
Average	Calculates the average value of a list of numbers.
Count	Calculates the number of values in a list.
Max	Finds the largest value in a list of numbers.
Min	Finds the smallest value in a list of numbers.

Can I perform calculations on several columns or rows of data at the same time?

Yes. Select the cells below or to the right of the cells that contain the numbers you want to include in the calculations. To select cells, see page 12. Then perform steps 2 and 3 on page 68.

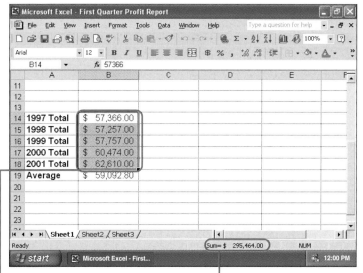

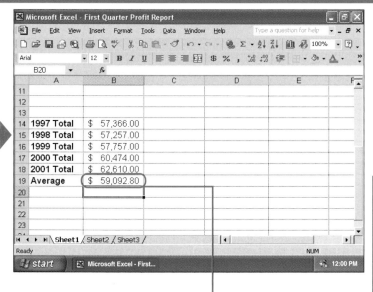

4 Press the Enter key to perform the calculation.

■ The result of the calculation appears.

QUICKLY ADD NUMBERS

You can quickly display the sum of a list of numbers without entering a formula into your worksheet.

1 Select the cells containing the numbers you want to add. To select cells, see page 12.

■ This area displays the sum of the cells you selected.

COPY A FORMULA

If you want to use the same formula several times in your worksheet, you can save time by copying the formula.

=B2+B3+B4   =C2+C3+C4   =D2+D3+D4

COPY A FORMULA—USING RELATIVE REFERENCES

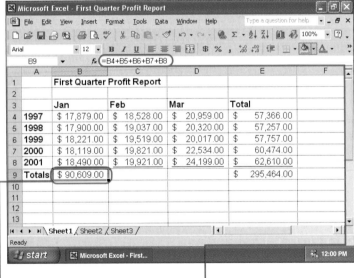

1 Enter the formula you want to copy to other cells. To enter a formula, see page 62.

2 Click the cell containing the formula you want to copy.

■ The formula bar displays the formula for the cell.

3 Position the mouse over the bottom right corner of the cell (changes to +).

4 Drag the mouse + over the cells you want to receive a copy of the formula.

What is a relative reference?

A relative reference is a cell reference that changes when you copy a formula.

	A	B	C
1	10	20	5
2	20	30	10
3	30	40	20
4	60	90	35
5			

=A1+A2+A3 ➡ =B1+B2+B3   =C1+C2+C3

This cell contains the formula =A1+A2+A3.

When you copy the formula to other cells in your worksheet, Excel automatically changes the cell references in the new formulas.

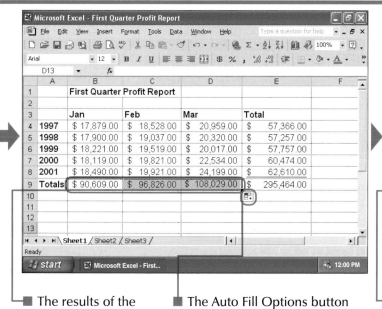

■ The results of the formulas appear.

■ The Auto Fill Options button also appears. You can click the button and then select an option to change the way Excel copies the formula. For example, you can specify that Excel should not use the formatting from the original cell.

5 To view one of the new formulas, click a cell that received a copy of the formula.

■ The formula bar displays the formula with the new cell references.

You can copy a formula to other cells in your worksheet to save time. If you do not want Excel to change a cell reference when you copy a formula, you can use an absolute reference.

	A	B	C	D
		R. Brown	J. Smith	K. Turner
		100	200	300
ission		= $A$7*B2	= $A$7*C2	= $A$7*D2

COPY A FORMULA—USING ABSOLUTE REFERENCES

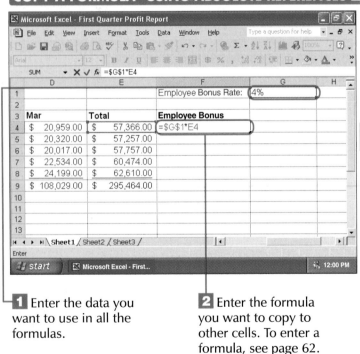

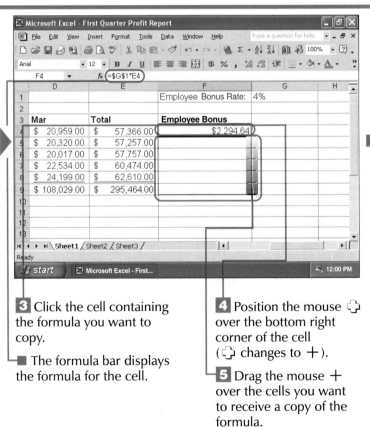

1 Enter the data you want to use in all the formulas.

2 Enter the formula you want to copy to other cells. To enter a formula, see page 62.

3 Click the cell containing the formula you want to copy.

■ The formula bar displays the formula for the cell.

4 Position the mouse over the bottom right corner of the cell (changes to +).

5 Drag the mouse + over the cells you want to receive a copy of the formula.

What is an absolute reference?

An absolute reference is a cell reference that does not change when you copy a formula. To make a cell reference absolute, type a dollar sign ($) before both the column letter and row number, such as **$A$7**.

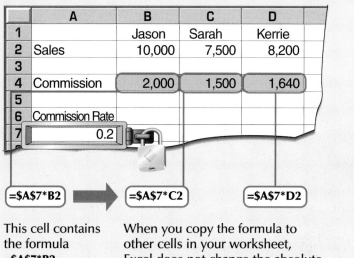

	A	B	C	D
1		Jason	Sarah	Kerrie
2	Sales	10,000	7,500	8,200
3				
4	Commission	2,000	1,500	1,640
5				
6	Commission Rate			
7	0.2			

=$A$7*B2 → =$A$7*C2   =$A$7*D2

This cell contains the formula **=$A$7*B2**.

When you copy the formula to other cells in your worksheet, Excel does not change the absolute reference in the new formulas.

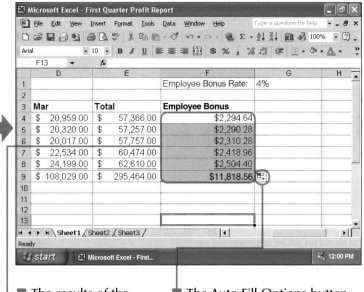

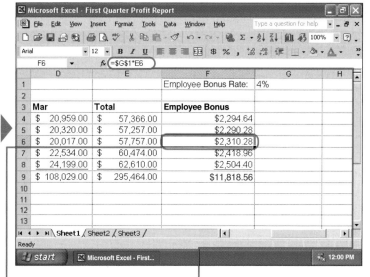

■ The results of the formulas appear.

■ The Auto Fill Options button also appears. You can click the button and then select an option to change the way Excel copies the formula. For example, you can specify that Excel should not use the formatting from the original cell.

6 To view one of the new formulas, click a cell that received a copy of the formula.

■ The formula bar displays the formula with the absolute reference and the new cell reference.

ERRORS IN FORMULAS

An error message appears when Excel cannot properly calculate or display the result of a formula.

Excel can help you correct common errors in your formulas. For information on correcting errors in formulas, see page 76.

	A	B	C
1	9924		
2	5521		
3			
4	#####		
5			
6			

#####

The column is too narrow to display the result of the calculation. You can change the column width to display the result. To change the column width, see page 48.

■ This cell contains the formula: =A1*A2

	A	B	C
1	50		
2			
3			
4	#DIV/0!		
5			
6			

#DIV/0!

The formula divides a number by zero (0). Excel considers a blank cell to have a value of zero.

■ This cell contains the formula: =A1/A2
=50/0

	A	B	C
1	10		
2	20		
3	30		
4	#NAME?		
5			
6			
7			

#NAME?

The formula contains a function name or cell reference Excel does not recognize.

■ This cell contains the formula: =AQ+A2+A3

In this example, the cell reference A1 was typed incorrectly.

	A	B	C
1	10		
2	20		
3	30		
4	#REF!		
5			
6			
7			

#REF!

The formula refers to a cell that is not valid.

■ This cell contains the formula: =A1+A2+A3

In this example, a row containing a cell used in the formula was deleted.

	A	B	C
1	10		
2	20		
3	January		
4	#VALUE!		
5			
6			
7			

#VALUE!

The formula refers to a cell that Excel cannot use in a calculation.

■ This cell contains the formula: =A1+A2+A3

In this example, a cell used in the formula contains text.

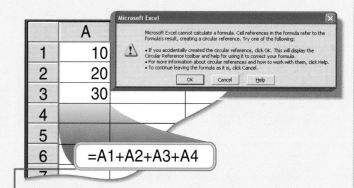

	A
1	10
2	20
3	30
4	
5	
6	=A1+A2+A3+A4
7	

Microsoft Excel

Microsoft Excel cannot calculate a formula. Cell references in the formula refer to the formula's result, creating a circular reference. Try one of the following:

- If you accidentally created the circular reference, click OK. This will display the Circular Reference toolbar and help for using it to correct your formula.
- For more information about circular references and how to work with them, click Help.
- To continue leaving the formula as it is, click Cancel.

[OK] [Cancel] [Help]

Circular Reference

A warning message appears when a formula refers to the cell containing the formula. This is called a circular reference.

■ This cell contains the formula: =A1+A2+A3+A4

CORRECT ERRORS IN FORMULAS

Excel can help you find and correct common errors in your formulas.

Excel checks your formulas for problems as you work and marks cells containing formulas with errors. For example, Excel marks cells that display an error message, such as #DIV/0!, #NAME?, #REF! or #VALUE!. For information on error messages, see page 74.

Errors in formulas are often the result of typing mistakes. You can edit a formula to correct an error or change the formula.

CORRECT ERRORS IN FORMULAS

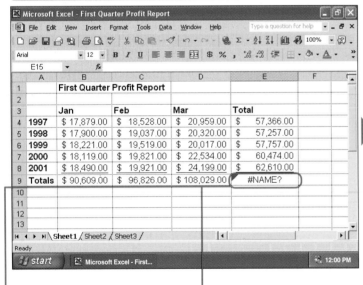

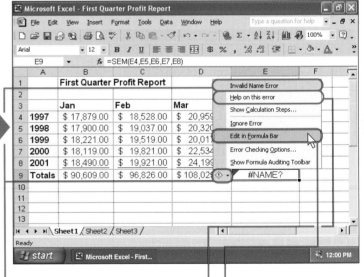

■ An error message appears in a cell when Excel cannot properly calculate the result of a formula.

■ A green triangle appears in the top left corner of a cell that contains an error Excel can help you correct.

1 To correct an error, click a cell displaying a green triangle.

■ The Trace Error button appears.

2 Click the Trace Error button to display a list of options.

■ This area describes the error.

3 To correct the error, click **Edit in Formula Bar**.

■ To view possible causes and solutions for the error in the Microsoft Excel Help window, click **Help on this error**.

Why does a green triangle appear in a cell that does not contain an error message?

Excel will display a green triangle in the top left corner of a cell containing a formula with one of the following problems.

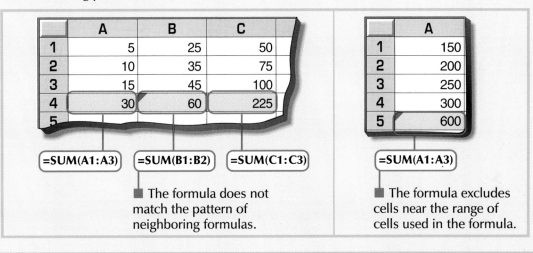

	A	B	C
1	5	25	50
2	10	35	75
3	15	45	100
4	30	60	225
5			

=SUM(A1:A3) =SUM(B1:B2) =SUM(C1:C3)

■ The formula does not match the pattern of neighboring formulas.

	A
1	150
2	200
3	250
4	300
5	600

=SUM(A1:A3)

■ The formula excludes cells near the range of cells used in the formula.

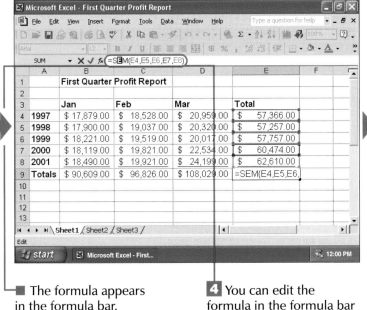

■ The formula appears in the formula bar.

4 You can edit the formula in the formula bar to correct the error. To edit a formula, perform steps **2** to **4** on page 63.

■ The result of the corrected formula appears in the cell.

■ You can repeat steps **1** to **4** to correct another error in your worksheet.

Central Division Standings

Pool A	Games	Goals	Wins	Losses	Ties	Points
Walt's Winners	6	15	4	1	1	9
The Chargers	6	13	3	2	1	7
Terry's Tigers	6	12	3	3	0	6
The Breakaways	6	10	1	3	2	4
The GO Team	6			4	1	3
Pool B	Games	Goals	Wins		Ties	Points
Brian's Boys		15	4		1	9
The Good Guys	6	15	4			8
Greg 'n' Gang		13	3			8
The Professionals	6	13	3			6
All The Way		12	4			4
Team Spirit	6	12	4			2
		10	3			
		9				

CHAPTER 5

CHANGE YOUR SCREEN DISPLAY

Are you interested in changing the way your worksheet appears on your screen? In this chapter, you will learn how to zoom in and out, hide columns and more.

Zoom Settings

Excel allows you to enlarge or reduce the display of data on your screen.

You can increase the zoom setting to view an area of your worksheet in more detail or decrease the zoom setting to view more of your worksheet at once.

ZOOM IN OR OUT

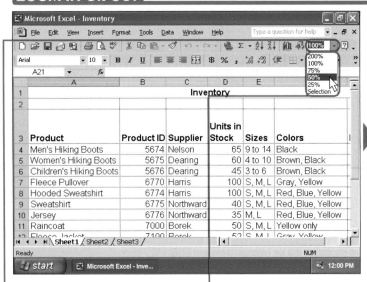

1 Click ▼ in this area to display a list of zoom settings.

Note: If the Zoom area is not displayed, click » on the Standard toolbar to display the area.

2 Click the zoom setting you want to use.

*Note: If you select cells before performing step 1, the **Selection** setting enlarges the selected cells to fill the window. To select cells, see page 12.*

■ The worksheet appears in the new zoom setting. You can edit the worksheet as usual.

■ Changing the zoom setting will not affect the way data appears on a printed page.

■ To return to the normal zoom setting, repeat steps **1** and **2**, selecting **100%** in step **2**.

DISPLAY FULL SCREEN

> You can display a larger working area by hiding parts of the Excel screen.

Using the full screen to view a worksheet is useful if you want to display as many cells as possible while you review and edit a large worksheet.

DISPLAY FULL SCREEN

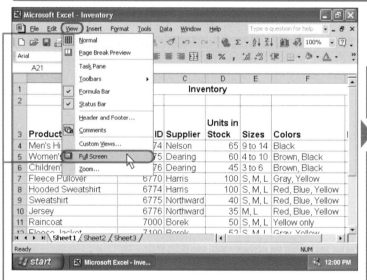

1 Click **View**.

2 Click **Full Screen**.

Note: If Full Screen does not appear on the menu, position the mouse ⍒ over the bottom of the menu to display all the menu options.

■ Excel hides parts of the screen to display a larger working area.

■ To once again display the hidden parts of the screen, click **Close Full Screen**.

Note: You can also repeat steps 1 and 2 to once again display the hidden parts of the screen.

Excel offers several toolbars that you can display or hide to suit your needs. Toolbars contain buttons that you can select to quickly perform common tasks.

When you first start Excel, the Standard and Formatting toolbars appear on your screen.

DISPLAY OR HIDE A TOOLBAR

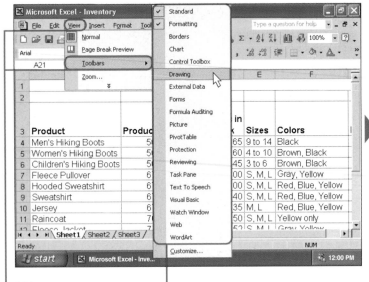

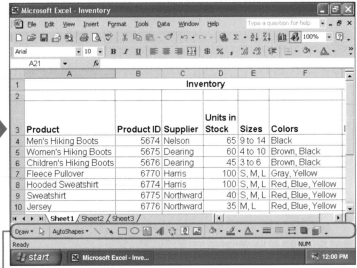

1 Click **View**.

2 Click **Toolbars**.

■ A list of toolbars appears. A check mark (✔) appears beside the name of each toolbar that is currently displayed.

3 Click the name of the toolbar you want to display or hide.

■ Excel displays or hides the toolbar you selected.

Note: A screen displaying fewer toolbars provides a larger and less cluttered working area.

MOVE A TOOLBAR

You can move a toolbar to the top, bottom, right or left edge of your screen.

You can move a toolbar to the same row as another toolbar or to its own row.

MOVE A TOOLBAR

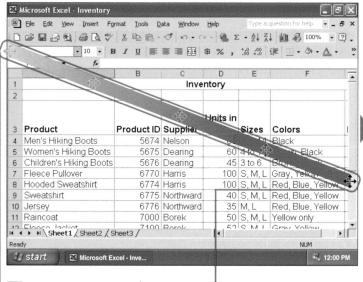

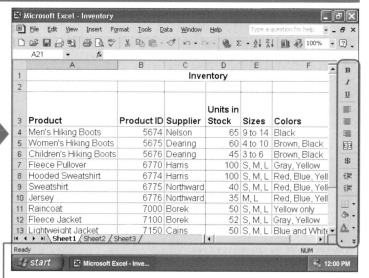

1 Position the mouse ⌖ over the move handle (▯) of the toolbar you want to move (⌖ changes to ✛).

2 Drag the toolbar to a new location.

■ The toolbar appears in the new location.

You can hide columns in your worksheet to reduce the amount of data displayed on your screen or temporarily remove confidential data.

You can hide a single column or multiple columns in your worksheet.

Hidden columns will not appear when you print your worksheet. This allows you to produce a printed copy of your worksheet that does not include unneeded or confidential data.

HIDE COLUMNS

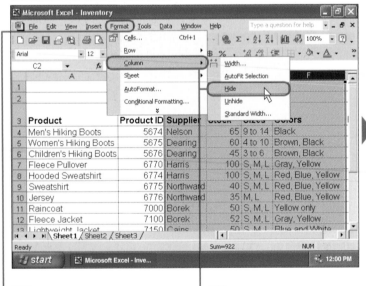

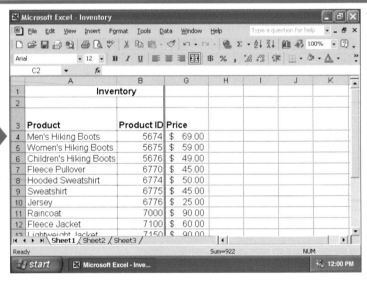

1 Select the columns you want to hide. To select columns, see page 13.

2 Click **Format**.

3 Click **Column**.

4 Click **Hide** to hide the columns.

■ The columns you selected disappear from your worksheet.

Will hiding columns affect the formulas and functions in my worksheet?

Hiding columns will not affect the results of formulas and functions in your worksheet. Excel will use data in the hidden columns to perform calculations even though the data is hidden from view. For information on formulas and functions, see pages 60 to 67.

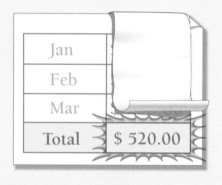

 Can I hide rows in my worksheet?

Yes. Select the rows you want to hide. To select rows, see page 13. Then perform steps 2 to 4 on page 84, selecting **Row** in step 3. To display the hidden rows, select the rows directly above and below the hidden rows. Then perform steps 2 to 4 on page 85, selecting **Row** in step 3.

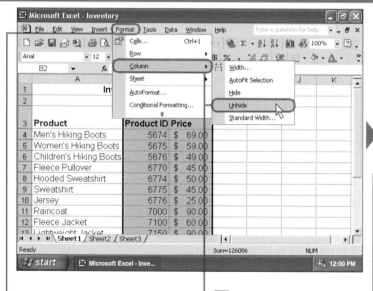

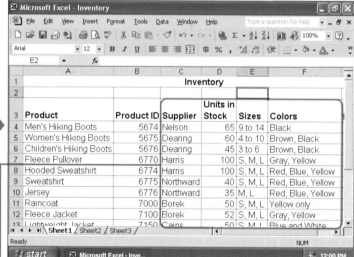

DISPLAY HIDDEN COLUMNS

1 Select the columns on each side of the hidden columns. To select columns, see page 13.

2 Click **Format**.

3 Click **Column**.

4 Click **Unhide** to display the hidden columns.

■ The hidden columns reappear in your worksheet.

■ To deselect cells, click any cell.

You can freeze rows and columns in your worksheet so they will not move. This allows you to keep row and column labels displayed on your screen as you move through a large worksheet.

FREEZE ROWS AND COLUMNS

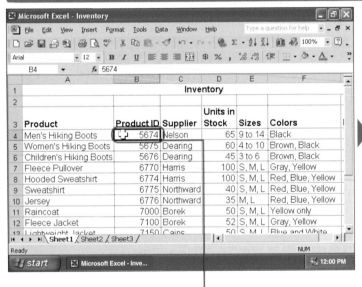

Excel will freeze the rows above and the columns to the left of the cell you select.

1 To select a cell, click the cell.

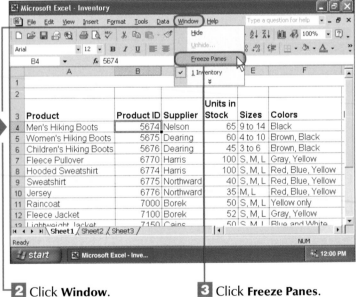

2 Click **Window**.

3 Click **Freeze Panes**.

Can I freeze only rows or only columns in my worksheet?

Yes. To freeze only rows, select the row below the rows you want to freeze. To freeze only columns, select the column to the right of the columns you want to freeze. Then perform steps 2 and 3 below. To select a row or column, see page 13.

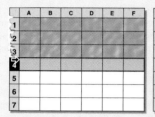

Freeze Only Rows

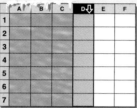

Freeze Only Columns

How do I unfreeze rows and columns in my worksheet?

When you no longer want to keep rows and columns frozen on your screen, perform steps 2 and 3 below, selecting **Unfreeze Panes** in step 3.

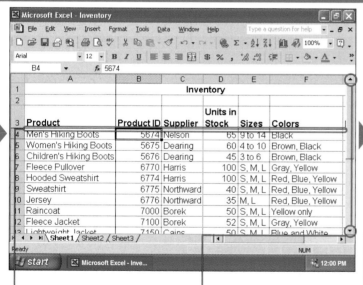

■ A horizontal line appears in your worksheet.

■ The rows above the horizontal line are frozen. These rows remain on your screen as you move through your worksheet.

■ To move through the rows below the horizontal line, click ▲ or ▼.

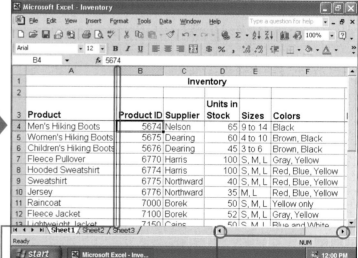

■ A vertical line appears in your worksheet.

■ The columns to the left of the vertical line are frozen. These columns remain on your screen as you move through your worksheet.

■ To move through the columns to the right of the vertical line, click ◄ or ►.

	Jan	Feb	Mar	Total
East	7	7	5	19
West	6	4	7	17
South	8	7	9	24
Total	21	18	21	60

Bold Italic Underline

CHAPTER 6

FORMAT YOUR WORKSHEETS

Would you like to improve the appearance of your worksheet? This chapter shows you how to change the color of data, add borders to cells and much more.

You can change the font of data to enhance the appearance of your worksheet.

CHANGE FONT OF DATA

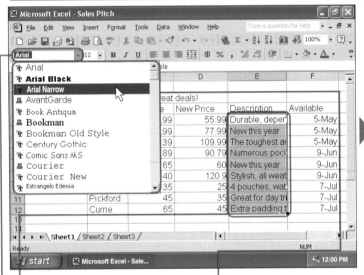

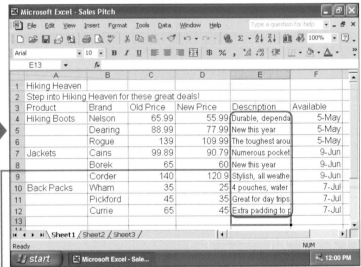

1 Select the cells containing the data you want to change to a different font. To select cells, see page 12.

2 Click ▼ in this area to display a list of the available fonts.

Note: If the Font area is not displayed, click ▸▸ on the Formatting toolbar to display the area.

3 Click the font you want to use.

■ The data changes to the font you selected.

■ To deselect cells, click any cell.

CHANGE SIZE OF DATA

You can increase or decrease the size of data in your worksheet.

Excel measures the size of data in points. There are approximately 72 points in one inch.

CHANGE SIZE OF DATA

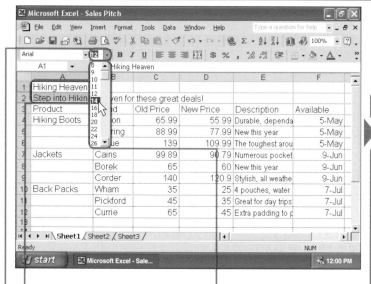

1 Select the cells containing the data you want to change to a new size. To select cells, see page 12.

2 Click ▾ in this area to display a list of the available sizes.

Note: If the Font Size area is not displayed, click ▸▸ on the Formatting toolbar to display the area.

3 Click the size you want to use.

■ The data changes to the size you selected.

■ To deselect cells, click any cell.

You can bold, italicize or underline data to emphasize data in your worksheet.

BOLD, ITALICIZE OR UNDERLINE DATA

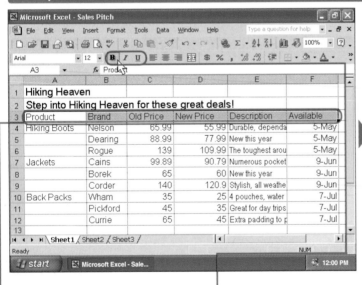

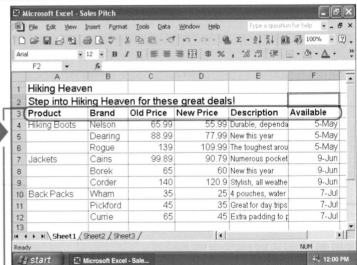

1 Select the cells containing the data you want to bold, italicize or underline. To select cells, see page 12.

2 Click one of the following buttons.

B Bold
I Italic
U Underline

Note: If the button you want is not displayed, click the arrow on the Formatting toolbar to display the button.

■ The data appears in the style you selected.

■ To deselect cells, click any cell.

■ To remove a bold, italic or underline style, repeat steps **1** and **2**.

You can change the way Excel aligns data within cells in your worksheet.

When you enter data into cells, Excel automatically left aligns text and right aligns numbers and dates.

CHANGE ALIGNMENT OF DATA

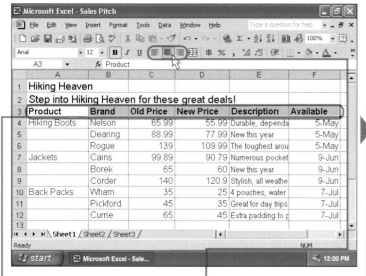

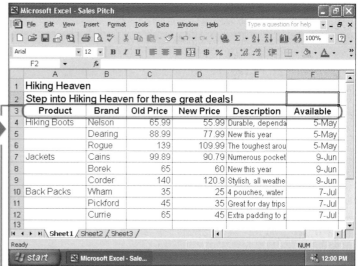

1 Select the cells containing the data you want to align differently. To select cells, see page 12.

2 Click one of the following buttons.

- ☰ Left align
- ☰ Center
- ☰ Right align

Note: If the button you want is not displayed, click » on the Formatting toolbar to display the button.

■ The data displays the new alignment.

■ To deselect cells, click any cell.

You can make data in your worksheet look more attractive by using various fonts, styles, sizes, effects and underlines.

CHANGE APPEARANCE OF DATA

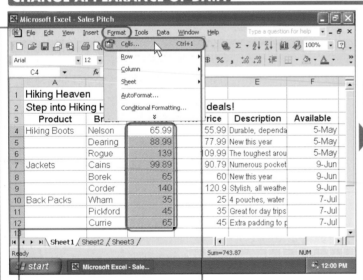

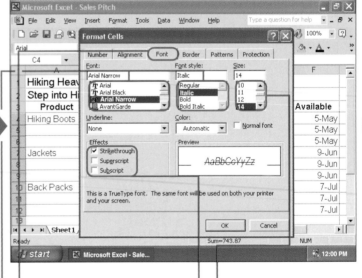

1 Select the cells containing the data you want to change. To select cells, see page 12.

2 Click **Format**.

3 Click **Cells**.

■ The Format Cells dialog box appears.

4 Click the **Font** tab.

5 To select a font for the data, click the font you want to use.

6 To select a style for the data, click the style you want to use.

7 To select a size for the data, click the size you want to use.

8 To select an effect for the data, click the effect you want to use (☐ changes to ☑).

What determines which fonts are available on my computer?

The fonts available on your computer depend on the programs installed on your computer. You can obtain additional fonts at computer stores and on the Internet.

What effects can I add to data in my worksheet?

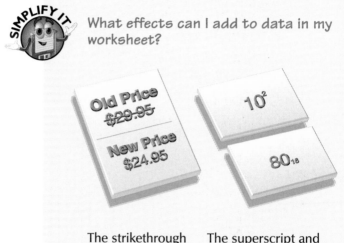

The strikethrough effect is useful for showing data that you have revised.

The superscript and subscript effects are useful for displaying mathematical formulas.

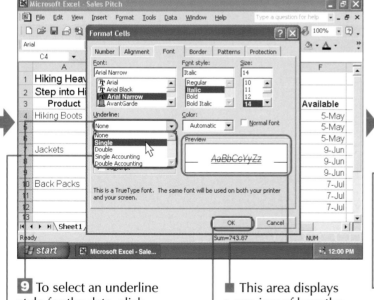

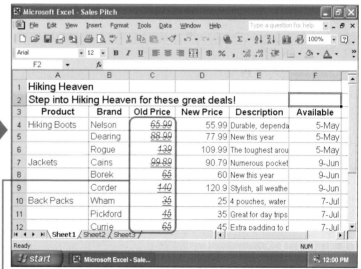

■ **9** To select an underline style for the data, click this area.

■ **10** Click the underline style you want to use.

■ This area displays a preview of how the data will appear in your worksheet.

■ **11** Click **OK** to apply your changes.

■ The data displays the changes.

■ To deselect cells, click any cell.

CHANGE DATA COLOR

You can change the color of data in your worksheet to draw attention to headings or important information.

CHANGE DATA COLOR

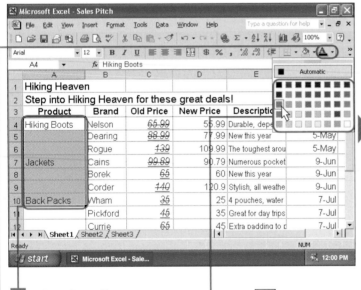

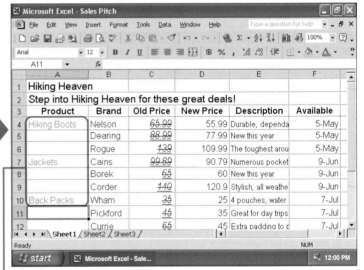

1 Select the cells containing the data you want to change to a different color. To select cells, see page 12.

2 Click ▾ in this area to display the available colors.

Note: If ▲▾ is not displayed, click ❯ on the Formatting toolbar to display the button.

3 Click the color you want to use.

■ The data appears in the color you selected.

■ To deselect cells, click any cell.

■ To return data to its original color, repeat steps **1** to **3**, selecting **Automatic** in step **3**.

You can add color to cells to make the cells stand out in your worksheet.

Adding color to cells is useful for marking data you want to review or verify later.

CHANGE CELL COLOR

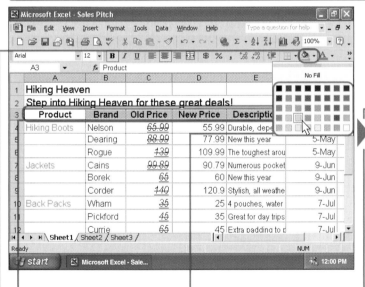

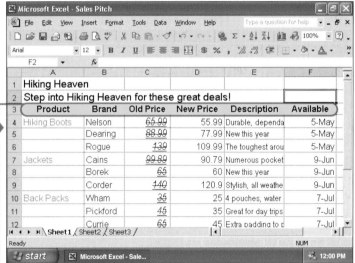

1 Select the cells you want to change to a different color. To select cells, see page 12.

2 Click ⋅ in this area to display the available colors.

Note: If ⬛⋅ is not displayed, click ⟩⟩ on the Formatting toolbar to display the button.

3 Click the color you want to use.

■ The cells appear in the color you selected.

■ To deselect cells, click any cell.

■ To remove color from cells, repeat steps **1** to **3**, selecting **No Fill** in step **3**.

INDENT DATA

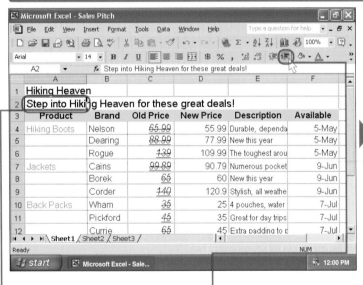

1 Select the cells containing the data you want to indent. To select cells, see page 12.

2 Click 📇 to indent the data.

Note: If 📇 is not displayed, click ⟩⟩ on the Formatting toolbar to display the button.

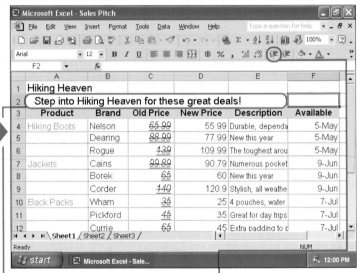

■ Excel indents the data.

■ You can repeat step **2** to further indent the data.

■ To decrease the indent, click 📇 .

Note: If 📇 is not displayed, click ⟩⟩ on the Formatting toolbar to display the button.

■ To deselect cells, click any cell.

> You can center data across several columns in your worksheet. This is useful for centering titles over your data.

CENTER DATA ACROSS COLUMNS

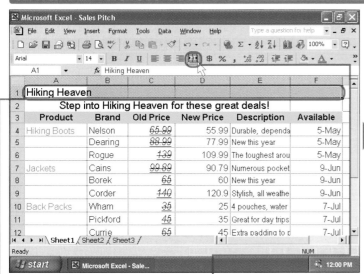

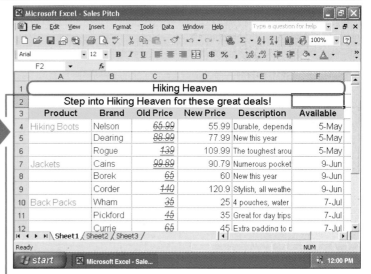

1 Select the cells you want to center the data across. To select cells, see page 12.

Note: The first cell you select should contain the data you want to center.

2 Click 📊 to center the data across the columns.

Note: If 📊 is not displayed, click 🔽 on the Formatting toolbar to display the button.

■ Excel centers the data across the columns.

■ If you no longer want to center the data across the columns, click the cell that contains the data and then repeat step **2**.

99

WRAP TEXT IN CELLS

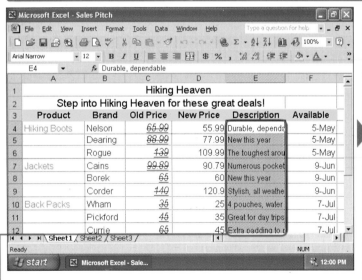

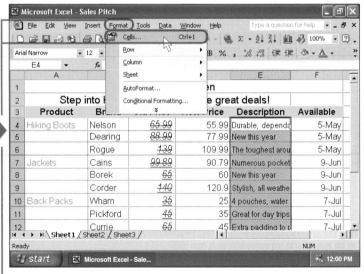

1 Select the cells containing the text you want to wrap. To select cells, see page 12.

2 Click **Format**.

3 Click **Cells**.

■ The Format Cells dialog box appears.

Can I display all the text in a cell without wrapping the text?

You can have Excel reduce the size of text to fit within a cell. Perform steps 1 to 6 below, selecting **Shrink to fit** in step 5 (☐ changes to ☑).

If you later change the width of the column, Excel will automatically adjust the size of the text to fit the new width.

Can I wrap text when entering text into a cell?

Yes. Type the text you want to display on the first line of the cell. Then press and hold down the Alt key as you press the Enter key to wrap to the next line. You can then type the text for the next line. You may need to increase the column width to properly see the wrapped text. To change the column width, see page 48.

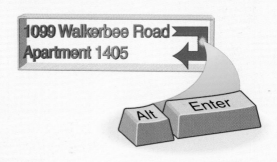

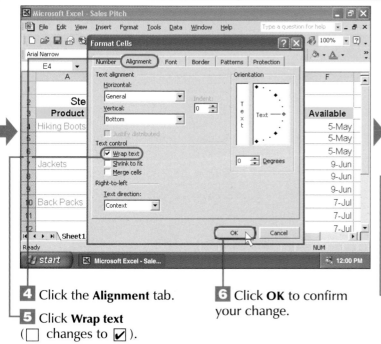

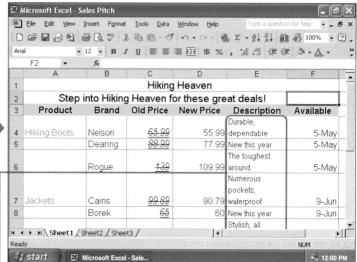

4 Click the **Alignment** tab.

5 Click **Wrap text** (☐ changes to ☑).

6 Click **OK** to confirm your change.

■ The text wraps within the cells you selected.

■ Excel automatically adjusts the row heights to fit the wrapped text.

■ To deselect cells, click any cell.

ADD BORDERS TO CELLS

You can add borders to cells to enhance the appearance of your worksheet.

Adding borders to cells is also useful if you want to divide your worksheet into sections.

ADD BORDERS TO CELLS

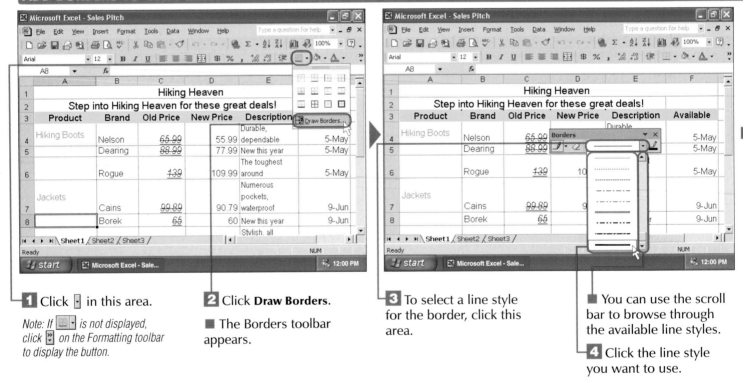

1 Click ⬝ in this area.

Note: If ⬛⬝ is not displayed, click �"⟩⟩⟩" on the Formatting toolbar to display the button.

2 Click **Draw Borders**.

■ The Borders toolbar appears.

3 To select a line style for the border, click this area.

■ You can use the scroll bar to browse through the available line styles.

4 Click the line style you want to use.

How can I quickly add borders to cells in my worksheet?

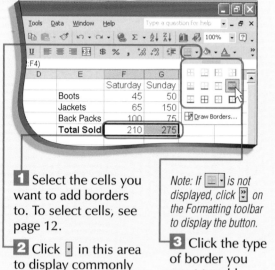

1 Select the cells you want to add borders to. To select cells, see page 12.

2 Click · in this area to display commonly used types of borders.

Note: If ▦ · is not displayed, click » on the Formatting toolbar to display the button.

3 Click the type of border you want to add.

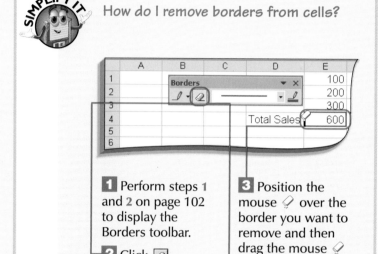

How do I remove borders from cells?

1 Perform steps 1 and 2 on page 102 to display the Borders toolbar.

2 Click ✎.

3 Position the mouse ✎ over the border you want to remove and then drag the mouse ✎ over the border.

■ When you finish removing borders, click ✎.

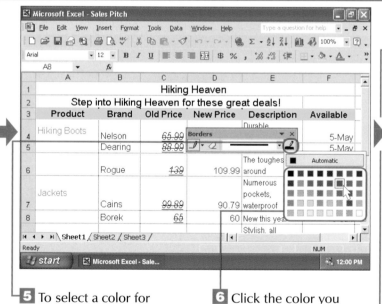

5 To select a color for the border, click ✎.

6 Click the color you want to use.

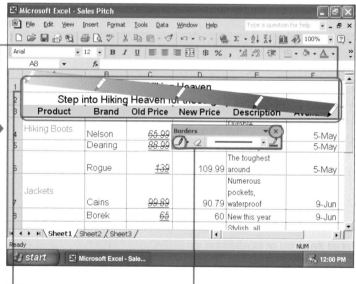

7 Position the mouse ✎ where you want the border to begin.

8 Drag the mouse ✎ to where you want the border to end.

■ The border appears.

■ You can repeat steps 7 and 8 for each border you want to add.

■ When you finish adding borders, click ✎.

■ To hide the Borders toolbar, click ✕.

103

CHANGE NUMBER FORMAT

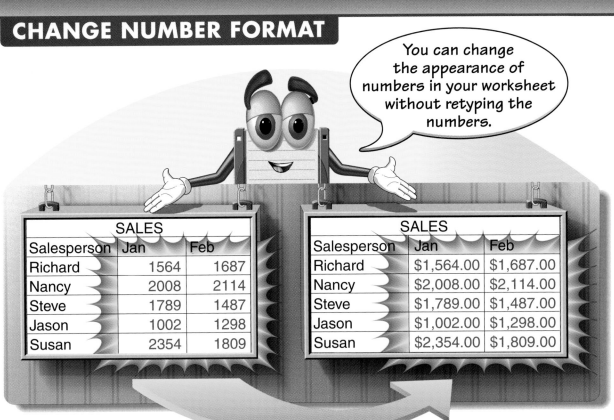

You can change the appearance of numbers in your worksheet without retyping the numbers.

SALES		
Salesperson	Jan	Feb
Richard	1564	1687
Nancy	2008	2114
Steve	1789	1487
Jason	1002	1298
Susan	2354	1809

SALES		
Salesperson	Jan	Feb
Richard	$1,564.00	$1,687.00
Nancy	$2,008.00	$2,114.00
Steve	$1,789.00	$1,487.00
Jason	$1,002.00	$1,298.00
Susan	$2,354.00	$1,809.00

When you change the format of numbers, you do not change the value of the numbers.

CHANGE NUMBER FORMAT

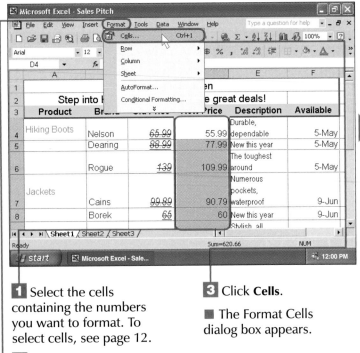

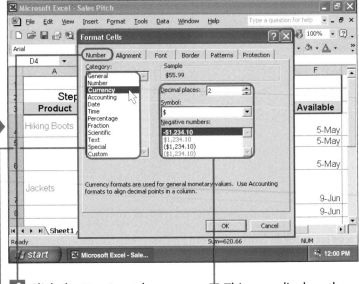

■1 Select the cells containing the numbers you want to format. To select cells, see page 12.

■2 Click **Format**.

■3 Click **Cells**.

■ The Format Cells dialog box appears.

■4 Click the **Number** tab.

■5 Click the category that describes the numbers in the cells you selected.

■ This area displays the options for the category you selected. The available options depend on the category you selected.

What categories are available for formatting numbers?

Category:	Description:	Example:
General	Applies no specific number format.	100
Number	Used to format numbers for general display.	100.00
Currency	Used to format monetary values.	$100.00
Accounting	Aligns the currency symbols and decimal points in a column of monetary values.	$ 100.00 $ 1200.00
Date	Used to format dates.	23-Apr-01
Time	Used to format times.	12:00 PM
Percentage	Used to format percentages.	25.00%
Fraction	Used to format fractions.	1/4
Scientific	Used to format numbers in scientific notation.	1.00E+02
Text	Treats numbers as text.	135 Hillcrest Street
Special	Used to format special numbers, such as ZIP codes.	02101
Custom	Allows you to apply your own number format.	3-45-678

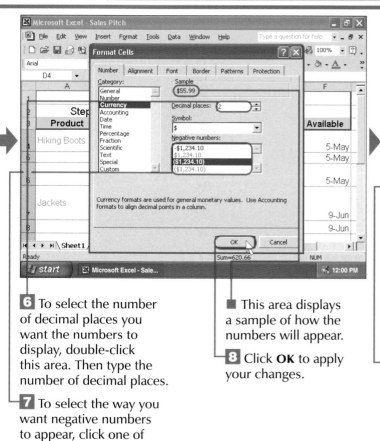

6 To select the number of decimal places you want the numbers to display, double-click this area. Then type the number of decimal places.

7 To select the way you want negative numbers to appear, click one of the available styles.

■ This area displays a sample of how the numbers will appear.

8 Click **OK** to apply your changes.

■ The numbers display the changes you specified.

QUICKLY FORMAT NUMBERS

1 Select the cells containing the numbers you want to format. To select cells, see page 12.

2 Click one of the following buttons.

$	Currency
%	Percent
,	Comma
	Add a decimal place
	Remove a decimal place

COPY FORMATTING

You can copy the formatting of a cell to make other cells in your worksheet look exactly the same.

You may want to copy the formatting of cells to make all the titles in your worksheet look the same. This will give the information in your worksheet a consistent appearance.

COPY FORMATTING

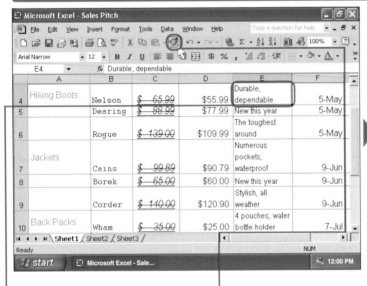

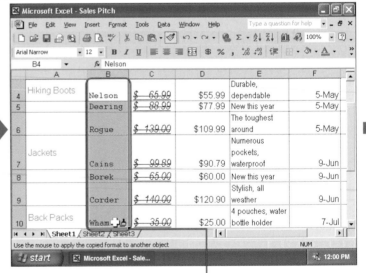

1 Click a cell that displays the formatting you want to copy to other cells.

2 Click ☑ to copy the formatting of the cell.

Note: If ☑ is not displayed, click » on the Standard toolbar to display the button.

■ The mouse ⬚ changes to ⬚ when over your worksheet.

3 Select the cells you want to display the formatting. To select cells, see page 12.

What types of formatting can I copy?

Number Formatting

Number formatting can include currency, percentage and date formats.

Data Formatting

Data formatting can include the font, size, color and alignment of data.

Cell Formatting

Cell formatting can include borders and colors.

How can I remove the formatting from cells?

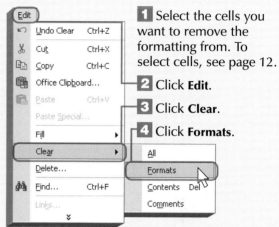

1 Select the cells you want to remove the formatting from. To select cells, see page 12.

2 Click **Edit**.

3 Click **Clear**.

4 Click **Formats**.

Note: If you remove the formatting from cells containing dates, the dates change to numbers. To once again display the dates, you must change the format of the cells to the Date format. For more information, see page 104.

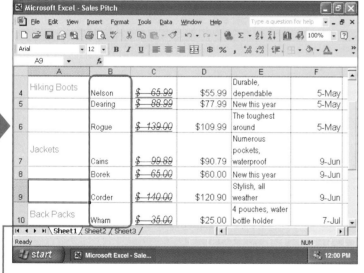

- The cells you selected display the formatting.

- To deselect cells, click any cell.

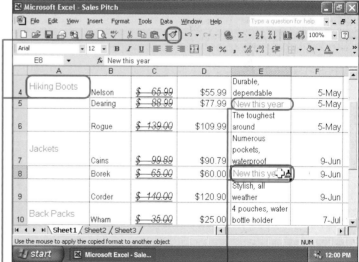

COPY FORMATTING TO SEVERAL AREAS

1 Click a cell that displays the formatting you want to copy to other cells.

2 Double-click to copy the formatting of the cell.

3 Select each group of cells you want to display the formatting.

4 When you finish copying the formatting, press the Esc key.

APPLY AN AUTOFORMAT

Excel offers many ready-to-use designs that you can choose from to give your worksheet a professional appearance.

APPLY AN AUTOFORMAT

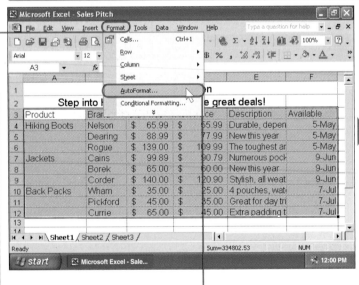

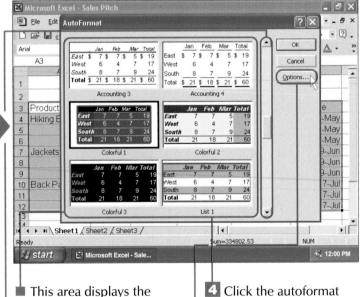

1 Select the cells you want to format. To select cells, see page 12.

2 Click **Format**.

3 Click **AutoFormat**.

■ The AutoFormat dialog box appears.

■ This area displays the available autoformats.

■ You can use the scroll bar to browse through the available autoformats.

4 Click the autoformat you want to use.

5 To view the formatting options for the autoformats, click **Options**.

What formatting will Excel apply to the cells in my worksheet?

Each autoformat includes a combination of formats, such as fonts, colors, borders, alignments and number styles. When you apply an autoformat, Excel may also adjust the column width and row height of the cells to best fit the data in the cells.

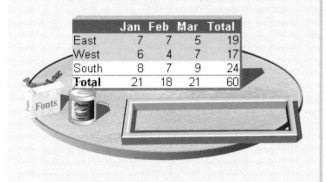

What happens if I add data to my worksheet after applying an autoformat?

If you enter data directly to the right or below the cells you applied an autoformat to, Excel may automatically format the new data. If Excel does not automatically format the new data, you can select all the cells you want to display the autoformat and then perform steps 2 to 7 below.

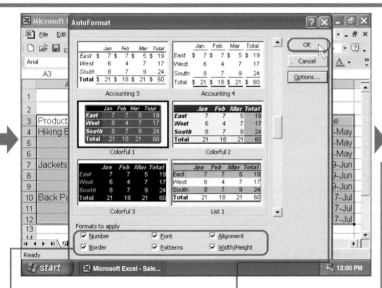

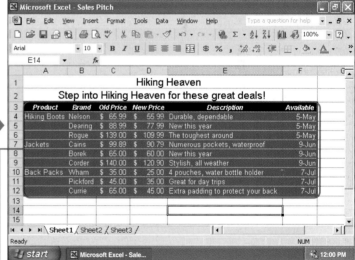

■ The formatting options appear in this area. A check mark (✔) beside an option indicates that Excel will apply the option to the cells.

6 You can click an option to add (☑) or remove (☐) a check mark.

7 Click **OK** to apply the autoformat to the cells you selected.

■ The cells display the autoformat you selected.

■ To deselect cells, click any cell.

■ To remove an autoformat, repeat steps 1 to 4, selecting **None** in step 4. Then perform step 7.

Portrait

UNITS SOLD

Apples — Jan, Feb
Oranges — Jan, Feb

Quarterly Earnings

2000	
1st Quarter	$ 260,050.00
2nd Quarter	$ 235,750.00
3rd Quarter	$ 256,455.00
4th Quarter	$ 234,000.00
Total	**$ 986,255.00**
2001	
1st Quarter	$ 278,350.00
2nd Quarter	$ 257,900.00
3rd Quarter	$ 300,500.00
4th Quarter	$ 340,350.00
Total	**$1,177,100.00**

Landscape

SALES

CHAPTER 7

PRINT YOUR WORKSHEETS

Are you ready to print your worksheet? In this chapter, you will learn how to preview your worksheet before printing and change the way your worksheet appears on a printed page.

Quarterly

2000	
1st Quarter	$
2nd Quarter	$
3rd Quarter	
4th Quarter	
Total	
2001	
1st Quarter	
2nd Quarter	
3rd Quarter	
4th Quarter	$ 340,350.00
Total	$1,177,100.00

You can use the Print Preview feature to see how your worksheet will look when printed. This allows you to confirm that the worksheet will print the way you expect.

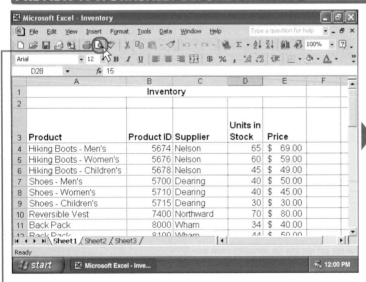

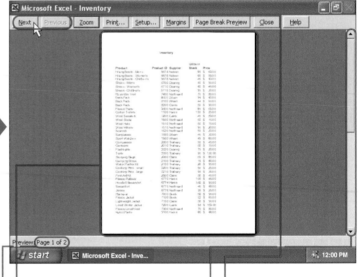

1 Click 🔍 to preview your worksheet before printing.

Note: If 🔍 is not displayed, click » on the Standard toolbar to display the button.

■ The Print Preview window appears.

■ This area displays a page from your worksheet.

■ This area indicates which page is displayed and the total number of pages in your worksheet.

2 If your worksheet contains more than one page, you can click **Next** or **Previous** to view the next or previous page.

■ You can also use the scroll bar to view other pages.

SIMPLIFY IT

Why does my worksheet appear in black and white in the Print Preview window?

If you are using a black-and-white printer, your worksheet will appear in black and white in the Print Preview window. If you are using a color printer, your worksheet will appear in color.

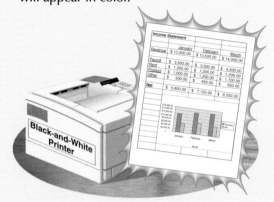

SIMPLIFY IT

Why don't the gridlines appear on my worksheet in the Print Preview window?

By default, Excel does not print the gridlines that appear around each cell in your worksheet. To print gridlines and change other printing options, see page 122.

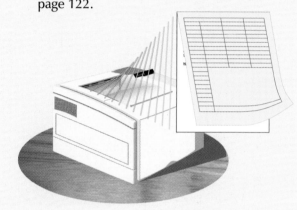

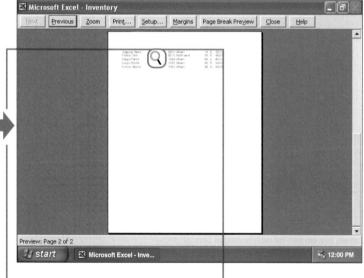

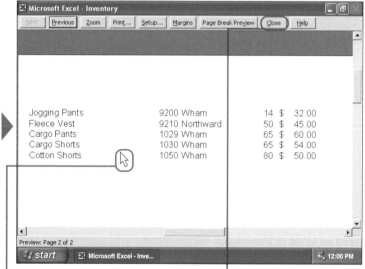

3 To magnify an area of the page, position the mouse ⟋ over the area you want to magnify (⟋ changes to ⚲).

4 Click the area to magnify the area.

■ A magnified view of the area appears.

5 To once again display the entire page, click anywhere on the page.

6 When you finish previewing your worksheet, click **Close** to close the Print Preview window.

You can produce a paper copy of the worksheet displayed on your screen.

Before printing a worksheet, make sure your printer is turned on and contains paper.

PRINT A WORKSHEET

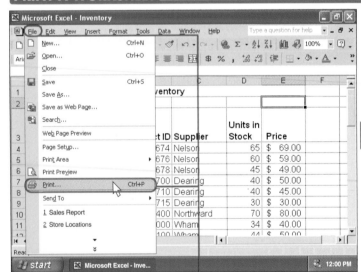

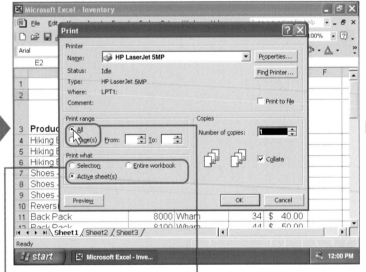

1 Click any cell in the worksheet you want to print.

■ To print only specific cells in the worksheet, select the cells you want to print. To select cells, see page 12.

2 Click **File**.

3 Click **Print**.

■ The Print dialog box appears.

4 Click the part of the workbook you want to print (○ changes to ⊙).

Note: For information on the parts of a workbook you can print, see the top of page 115.

5 If the part of the workbook you selected to print contains more than one page, click an option to specify which pages you want to print (○ changes to ⊙).

All - Prints every page.

Page(s) - Prints the pages you specify.

Which parts of a workbook can I print?

Excel allows you to specify the part of a workbook you want to print. Each workbook is divided into several worksheets.

For information on using multiple worksheets in a workbook, see pages 134 to 143.

Selection

Prints the cells you selected.

Active sheet(s)

Prints the displayed worksheet.

Entire workbook

Prints every worksheet in the workbook.

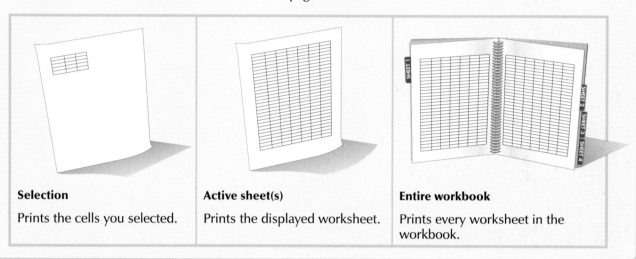

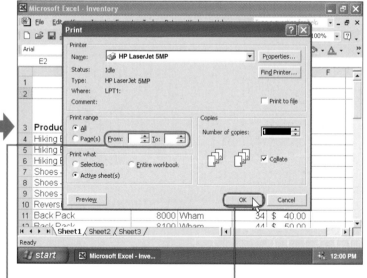

■ If you selected **Page(s)** in step **5**, type the number of the first page you want to print. Press the Tab key and then type the number of the last page you want to print.

6 Click **OK**.

QUICKLY PRINT DISPLAYED WORKSHEET

1 Click 🖨 to quickly print the worksheet displayed on your screen.

Note: If 🖨 is not displayed, click ⯈ on the Standard toolbar to display the button.

SET A PRINT AREA

If you always print the same area of your worksheet, you can set a print area to quickly print the data. Excel will print only the data in the print area.

If you have not set a print area for your worksheet, Excel will print the entire worksheet.

SET A PRINT AREA

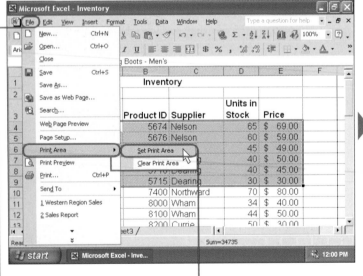

1 Select the cells containing the data you want to include in the print area. To select cells, see page 12.

2 Click **File**.

3 Click **Print Area**.

4 Click **Set Print Area**.

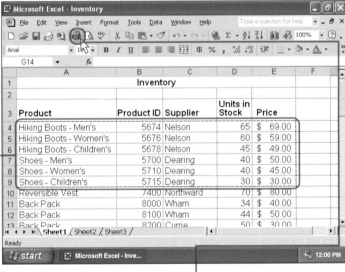

■ A dashed line appears around the cells you selected.

■ To deselect cells, click any cell.

PRINT A PRINT AREA

1 Click 🖨 to print the data in the print area at any time.

Can I include multiple groups of cells in a print area?

Yes. Including multiple groups of cells in a print area is useful when you want to print data from several sections of a large worksheet. When you set a print area that includes multiple groups of cells, Excel prints each group of cells on a different page. To select multiple groups of cells, see page 12.

How do I print other data in my worksheet after I set a print area?

You can temporarily override a print area you have set and print other data in your worksheet. Select the cells containing the data you want to print and then perform steps 2 to 6 starting on page 114, choosing **Selection** in step 4 (○ changes to ⊙).

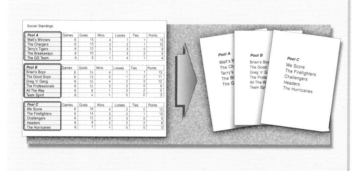

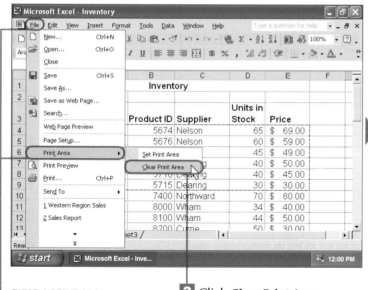

CLEAR A PRINT AREA

1 Click **File**.

2 Click **Print Area**.

3 Click **Clear Print Area** to clear the print area from your worksheet.

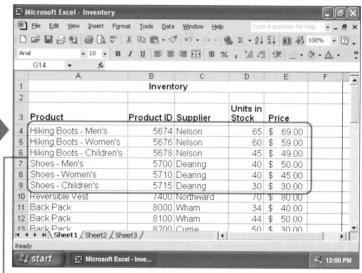

■ The dashed line disappears from your worksheet.

You can center data horizontally and vertically on a printed page.

Centering data on a printed page will not affect the way your worksheet appears on your screen.

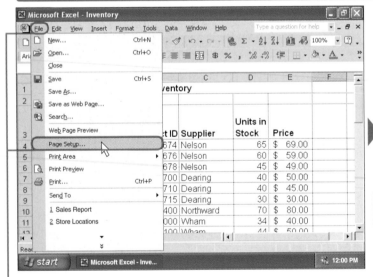

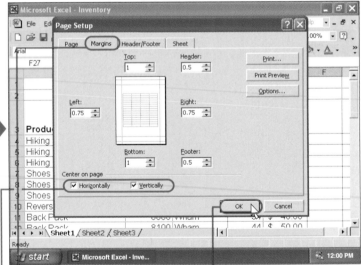

1 Click **File**.

2 Click **Page Setup**.

■ The Page Setup dialog box appears.

3 Click the **Margins** tab.

4 Click the way you want to center the data (☐ changes to ☑). You can select both options to horizontally and vertically center the data.

5 Click **OK** to confirm your change.

Note: You can use the Print Preview feature to see how your worksheet will appear on a printed page. For information on using the Print Preview feature, see page 112.

118

CHANGE PAGE ORIENTATION

You can change the page orientation to change the way your worksheet appears on a printed page.

Excel automatically prints worksheets in the portrait orientation. The landscape orientation is useful when you want a wide worksheet to fit on one printed page.

Changing the page orientation will not affect the way your worksheet appears on your screen.

CHANGE PAGE ORIENTATION

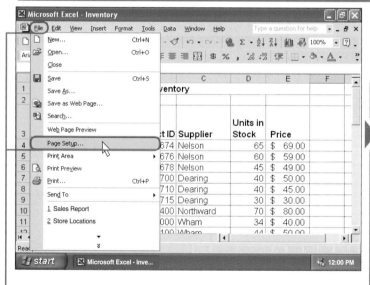

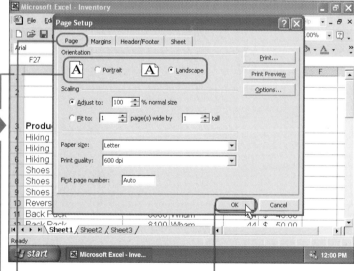

■ 1 Click **File**.

■ 2 Click **Page Setup**.

■ The Page Setup dialog box appears.

■ 3 Click the **Page** tab.

■ 4 Click the orientation you want to use (○ changes to ◉).

■ 5 Click **OK** to confirm your change.

Note: You can use the Print Preview feature to see how your worksheet will appear on a printed page. For information on using the Print Preview feature, see page 112.

119

CHANGE MARGINS

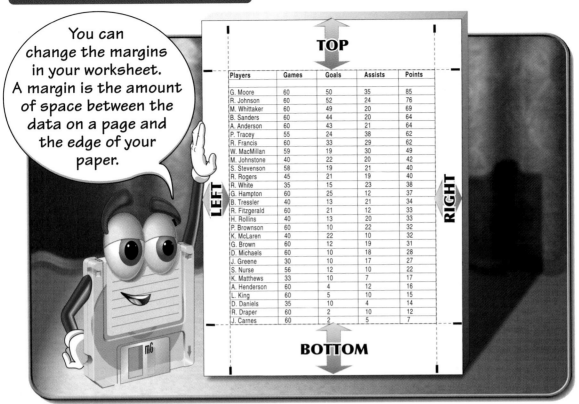

You can change the margins in your worksheet. A margin is the amount of space between the data on a page and the edge of your paper.

Changing the margins allows you to adjust the amount of information that can fit on a page. You may want to change the margins to accommodate letterhead or other specialty paper.

Changing the margins will not affect the way your worksheet appears on your screen.

CHANGE MARGINS

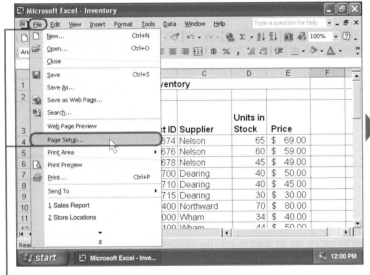

1 Click **File**.

2 Click **Page Setup**.

■ The Page Setup dialog box appears.

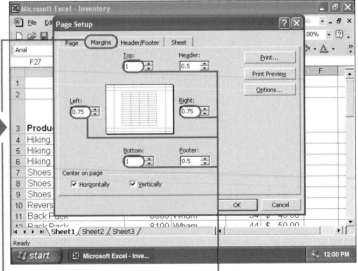

3 Click the **Margins** tab.

■ These areas display the current margins for your worksheet.

Note: By default, Excel sets the top and bottom margins to 1 inch and the left and right margins to 0.75 inches.

120

Is there another way to change the margins in my worksheet?

Yes. You can use the Print Preview feature to change the margins in your worksheet.

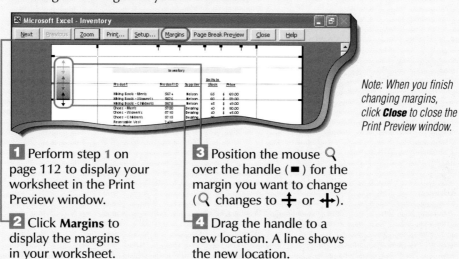

*Note: When you finish changing margins, click **Close** to close the Print Preview window.*

1 Perform step **1** on page 112 to display your worksheet in the Print Preview window.

2 Click **Margins** to display the margins in your worksheet.

3 Position the mouse ⌕ over the handle (■) for the margin you want to change (⌕ changes to ⊕ or ↔).

4 Drag the handle to a new location. A line shows the new location.

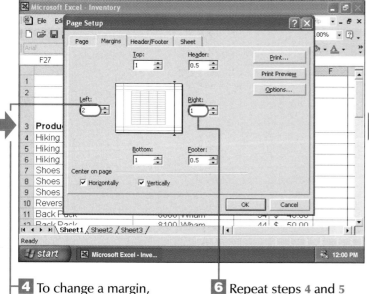

4 To change a margin, double-click in the box for the margin you want to change.

5 Type a new margin in inches.

6 Repeat steps **4** and **5** for each margin you want to change.

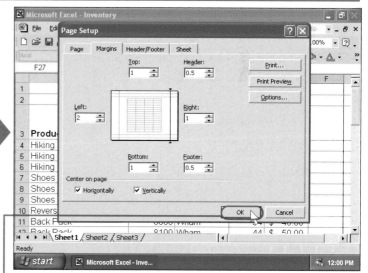

7 Click **OK** to confirm your changes.

Note: You can use the Print Preview feature to see how your worksheet will appear on a printed page. For information on using the Print Preview feature, see page 112.

121

CHANGE PRINT OPTIONS

You can use the print options that Excel offers to change the way your worksheet appears on a printed page.

Changing the print options will not affect the way your worksheet appears on your screen.

CHANGE PRINT OPTIONS

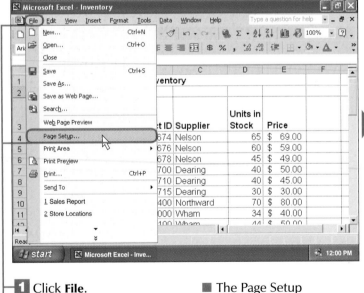

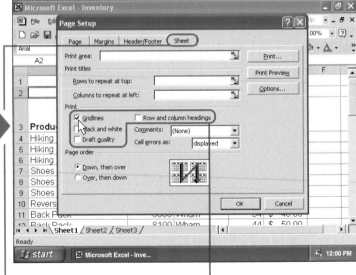

1 Click **File**.

2 Click **Page Setup**.

■ The Page Setup dialog box appears.

3 Click the **Sheet** tab.

4 Click each print option you want to use (☐ changes to ☑).

What are some of the print options Excel offers?

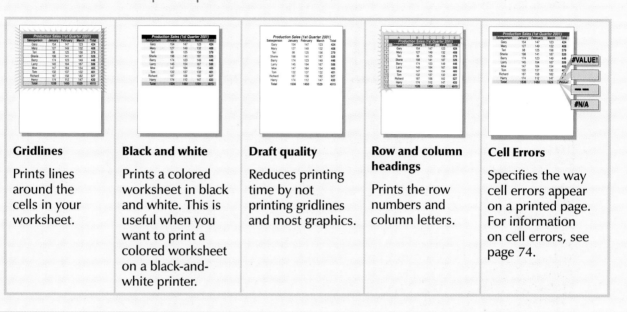

Gridlines

Prints lines around the cells in your worksheet.

Black and white

Prints a colored worksheet in black and white. This is useful when you want to print a colored worksheet on a black-and-white printer.

Draft quality

Reduces printing time by not printing gridlines and most graphics.

Row and column headings

Prints the row numbers and column letters.

Cell Errors

Specifies the way cell errors appear on a printed page. For information on cell errors, see page 74.

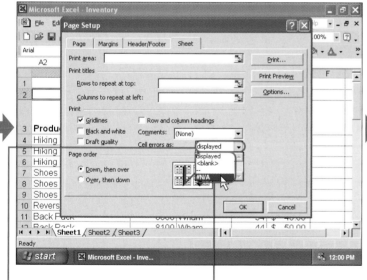

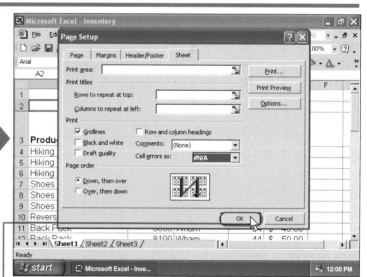

■ By default, Excel will print any cell errors that appear in your worksheet.

5 To specify how you want cell errors to appear when you print your worksheet, click this area.

6 Click the way you want cell errors to appear.

7 Click **OK** to confirm your changes.

Note: You can use the Print Preview feature to see how your worksheet will appear on a printed page. For information on using the Print Preview feature, see page 112.

You can insert a page break to start a new page at a specific location in your worksheet. A page break indicates where one page ends and another begins.

INSERT A PAGE BREAK

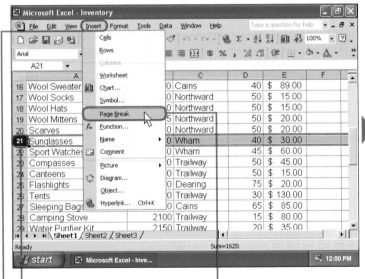

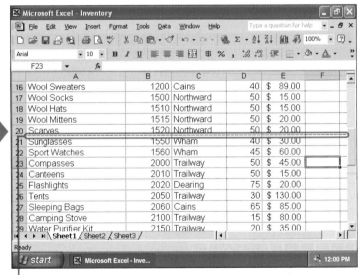

1 To select the row or column you want to appear at the beginning of the new page, click the heading of the row or column.

2 Click **Insert**.

3 Click **Page Break**.

Note: If Page Break does not appear on the menu, position the mouse ⅄ over the bottom of the menu to display all the menu options.

■ A dashed line appears on your screen. This line indicates where one page ends and another begins.

■ The dashed line will not appear when you print your worksheet.

■ To deselect a row or column, click any cell.

Will Excel ever insert page breaks automatically?

When you fill a page with data, Excel automatically inserts a page break to start a new page.

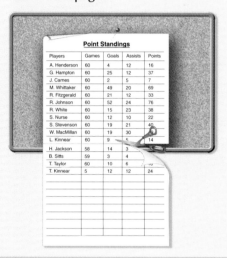

How do I delete a page break I inserted into my worksheet?

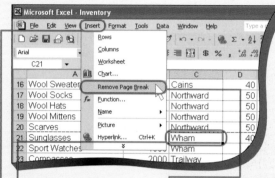

1 Click a cell directly below or directly to the right of the page break line you want to delete.

2 Click **Insert**.

3 Click **Remove Page Break** to delete the page break.

Note: If Remove Page Break does not appear on the menu, position the mouse ⤵ over the bottom of the menu to display all the menu options.

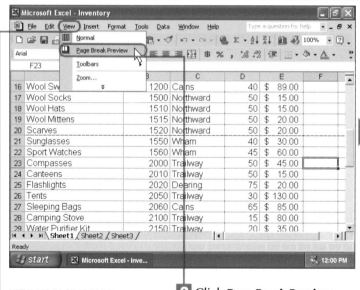

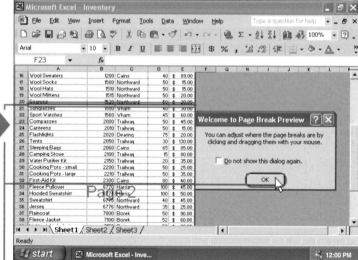

VIEW ALL PAGE BREAKS

1 Click **View**.

2 Click **Page Break Preview** to display all the page breaks in your worksheet.

■ A Welcome dialog box appears.

3 Click **OK** to close the dialog box.

■ A solid blue line shows the location of a page break you inserted into your worksheet.

Note: A dashed blue line shows the location of a page break Excel inserted for you.

■ To return to the normal view at any time, repeat steps **1** and **2**, selecting **Normal** in step **2**.

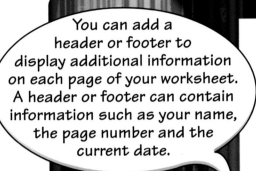

You can add a header or footer to display additional information on each page of your worksheet. A header or footer can contain information such as your name, the page number and the current date.

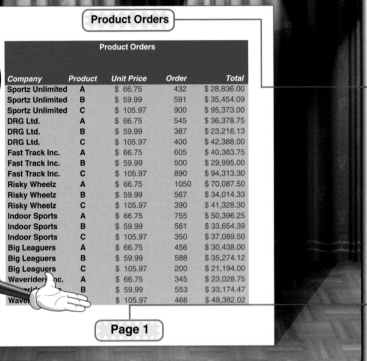

■ A **header** appears at the top of each printed page.

■ A **footer** appears at the bottom of each printed page.

ADD A HEADER OR FOOTER

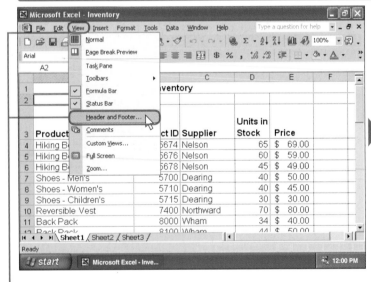

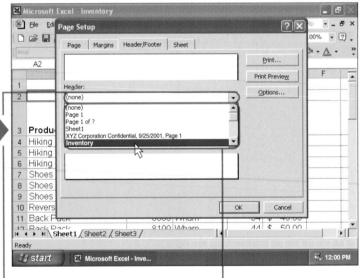

1 Click **View**.

2 Click **Header and Footer**.

Note: If Header and Footer does not appear on the menu, position the mouse over the bottom of the menu to display all the menu options.

■ The Page Setup dialog box appears.

3 To view a list of available headers, click this area.

4 Click the header you want to use.

SIMPLIFY IT

Can I see how a header or footer will look before I print my worksheet?

You can use the Print Preview feature to see how a header or footer will look before you print your worksheet. For information on using the Print Preview feature, see page 112.

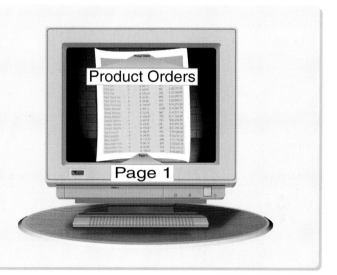

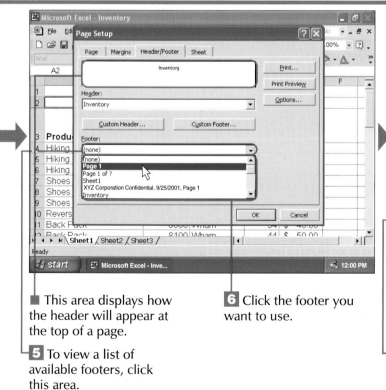

■ This area displays how the header will appear at the top of a page.

5 To view a list of available footers, click this area.

6 Click the footer you want to use.

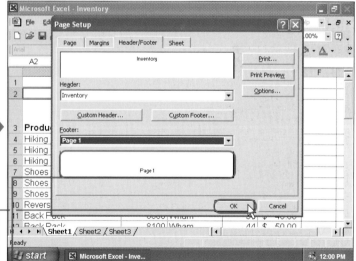

■ This area displays how the footer will appear at the bottom of a page.

7 Click **OK** to add the header or footer to your worksheet.

■ To remove a header or footer from your worksheet, repeat steps **1** to **7**, selecting (**none**) in step **4** or step **6**.

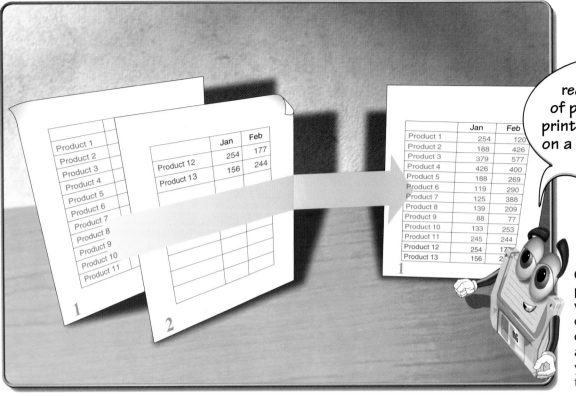

You can reduce the size of printed data to print your worksheet on a specific number of pages.

Changing the size of printed data is useful when the last page of your worksheet contains a small amount of data that you want to fit on the previous page.

CHANGE SIZE OF PRINTED DATA

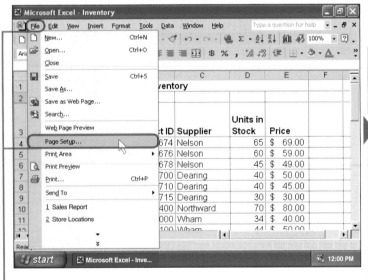

1 Click **File**.

2 Click **Page Setup**.

■ The Page Setup dialog box appears.

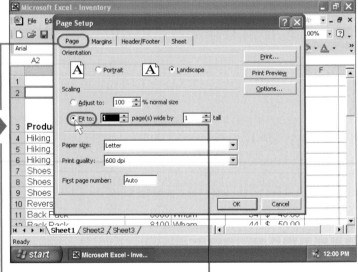

3 Click the **Page** tab.

4 Click **Fit to** to fit the worksheet on a specific number of pages (○ changes to ◉).

What should I consider when changing the size of printed data?

When specifying the number of pages you want to print data across and down, you must consider the amount of data you need to print. If you try to fit the data on too few pages, the data may become too small to read.

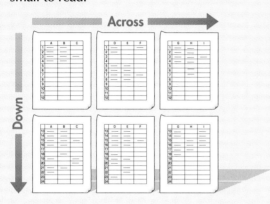

Why did the page breaks in my worksheet disappear when I changed the size of printed data?

When you change the size of printed data, Excel ignores any page breaks you have inserted into your worksheet. This allows Excel to fit the worksheet data on the number of pages you specify. For information on inserting page breaks, see page 124.

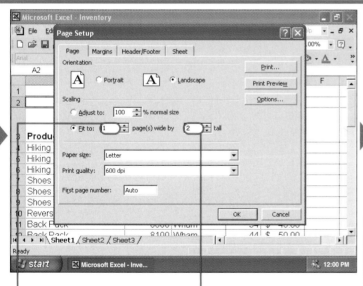

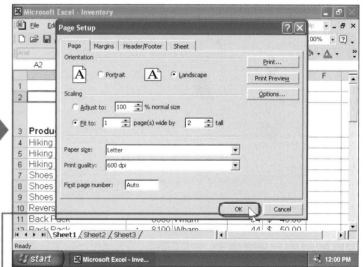

5 Type the number of pages you want the data to print across.

6 Press the Tab key and then type the number of pages you want the data to print down.

7 Click **OK** to confirm your changes.

■ Excel will change the size of the printed data to fit on the number of pages you specified.

Note: You can use the Print Preview feature to see how your worksheet will appear on a printed page. For information on using the Print Preview feature, see page 112.

129

REPEAT LABELS ON PRINTED PAGES

You can display the same row or column labels on every printed page of a worksheet. This can help you review worksheets that print on several pages.

Repeat Row Labels

Repeat Column Labels

REPEAT LABELS ON PRINTED PAGES

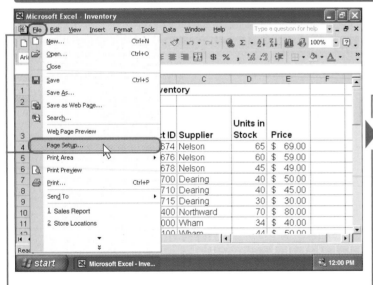

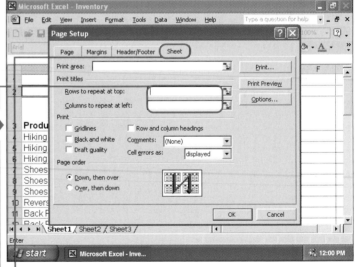

1 Click **File**.

2 Click **Page Setup**.

■ The Page Setup dialog box appears.

3 Click the **Sheet** tab.

4 Click the area beside one of the following options.

Rows to repeat at top
Repeat labels across top of each page.

Columns to repeat at left
Repeat labels down left side of each page.

Can I see how the repeated labels will look before I print my worksheet?

You can use the Print Preview feature to see how the repeated labels will look before you print your worksheet. For information on using the Print Preview feature, see page 112.

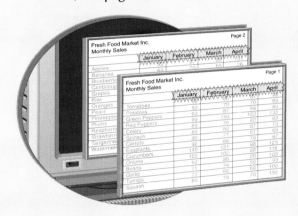

How *do* I stop repeating labels on printed pages?

Perform steps 1 to 4 below, except in step 4, drag the mouse I over the text in the area beside the appropriate option until you highlight the text. Press the Delete key to remove the text from the area and then perform step 7.

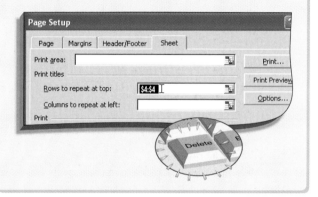

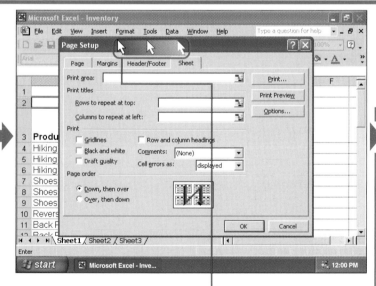

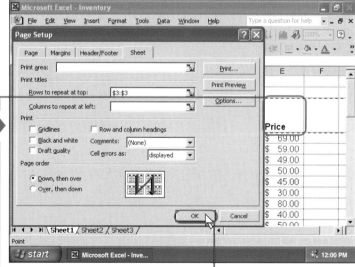

■ If the Page Setup dialog box covers the row or column containing the labels you want to repeat, you can move the dialog box to a new location.

5 To move the dialog box, position the mouse ⌖ over the title bar and then drag the dialog box to a new location.

6 Click one cell in the row or column containing the labels you want to repeat.

■ A moving outline appears around the row or column.

7 Click **OK** to confirm your changes.

WORKSHEET 1

Sportz Inc.

SALES REPORT

	January	February	March	Total	Commission
			$49,800.00	$146,400.00	$2,928.00
Jim	$51,000.00	$45,600.00	$40,100.00	$112,300.00	$2,246.00
Mary	$36,700.00	$35,500.00	$27,800.00	$83,500.00	$1,670.00
Arthur	$30,200.00	$25,500.00	$44,000.00	$133,700.00	$2,674.00
Nancy	$45,800.00	$43,900.00			
TOTAL SALES	$163,700.00	$150,500.00	$161,700.00	$475,900.00	

Commission Rate
0.02

WORKSHEET 2

	January	February	March	Total	Commission
			$49,800.00	$146,400.00	$2,928.00
Jim	$51,000.00	$45,600.00	$40,100.00	$112,300.00	$2,246.00
Mary	$36,700.00	$35,500.00	$27,800.00	$83,500.00	$1,670.00
Arthur	$30,200.00	$25,500.00	$44,000.00	$133,700.00	$2,674.00
Nancy	$45,800.00	$43,900.00			
TOTAL SALES	$163,700.00	$150,500.00	$161,700.00	$475,900.00	

INVENTORY REVENUE EXPENSES
xpenses

CHAPTER 8

WORK WITH MULTIPLE WORKSHEETS

Do you want to work with more than one worksheet at a time? This chapter teaches you how to switch between worksheets, move or copy data between worksheets, color worksheet tabs and more.

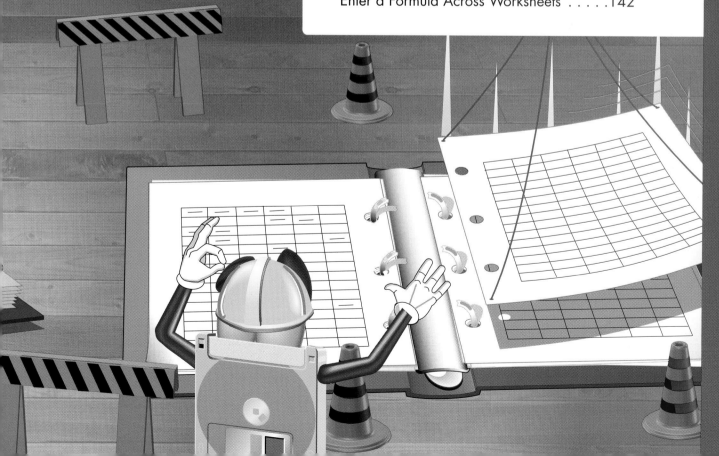

A workbook contains several worksheets. You can easily switch from one worksheet to another.

Worksheets can help you organize information in your workbook. For example, you can store information for each division of a company on a separate worksheet.

SWITCH BETWEEN WORKSHEETS

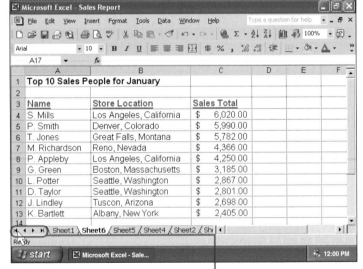

■ This area displays a tab for each worksheet in your workbook. The displayed worksheet has a white tab.

1 Click the tab for the worksheet you want to display.

■ The worksheet you selected appears. The contents of the other worksheets in your workbook are hidden behind the displayed worksheet.

BROWSE THROUGH WORKSHEET TABS

■ If you have many worksheets in your workbook, you may not be able to see all the worksheet tabs.

Note: To insert additional worksheets, see page 136.

1 Click one of the following buttons to browse through the worksheet tabs.

◄ Display first tab
◄ Display previous tab
► Display next tab
► Display last tab

RENAME A WORKSHEET

RENAME A WORKSHEET

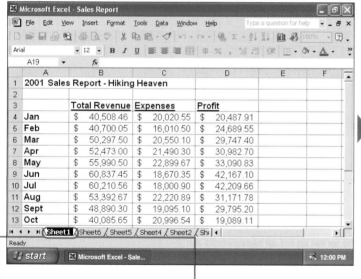 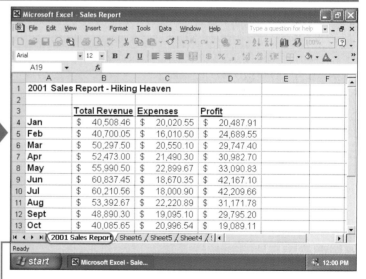

1 Double-click the tab for the worksheet you want to rename.

■ The name of the worksheet is highlighted.

2 Type a new name for the worksheet and then press the Enter key.

Note: A worksheet name can contain up to 31 characters, including spaces.

RENAME A WORKSHEET

You can insert a new worksheet to include additional information in your workbook.

Each workbook you create automatically contains three worksheets. You can insert as many new worksheets as you need.

INSERT A WORKSHEET

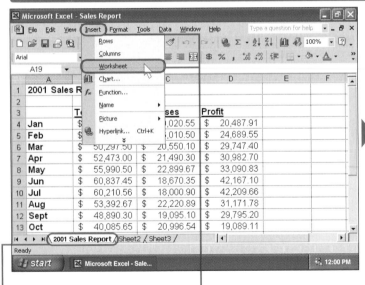

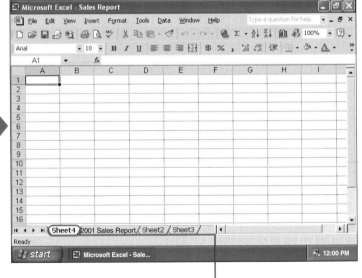

1 Click the tab for the worksheet you want to appear after the new worksheet.

2 Click **Insert**.

3 Click **Worksheet**.

■ The new worksheet appears.

■ Excel displays a tab for the new worksheet.

You can permanently remove a worksheet you no longer need from your workbook.

DELETE A WORKSHEET

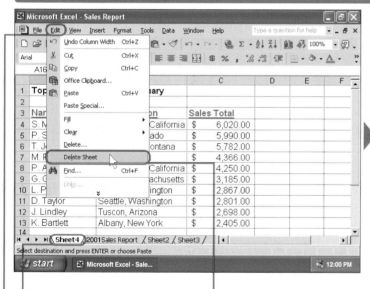

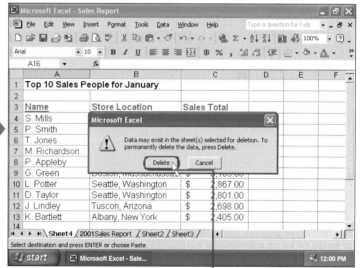

1 Click the tab for the worksheet you want to delete.

2 Click **Edit**.

3 Click **Delete Sheet**.

Note: If Delete Sheet does not appear on the menu, position the mouse ⬚ over the bottom of the menu to display all the menu options.

■ A warning dialog box may appear, stating that Excel will permanently delete the data in the worksheet.

4 Click **Delete** to permanently delete the worksheet.

You can move a worksheet to a new location in your workbook. This allows you to reorganize the data in your workbook.

MOVE A WORKSHEET

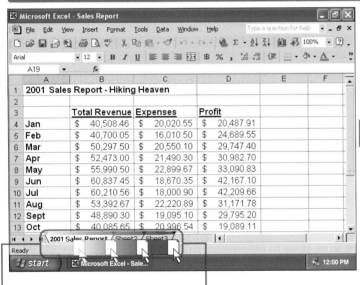

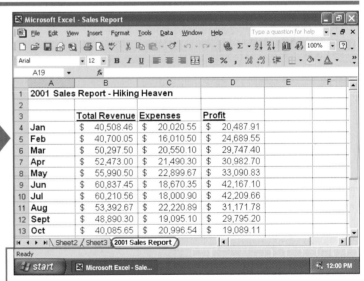

1 Position the mouse ⟍ over the tab for the worksheet you want to move.

2 Drag the worksheet to a new location.

■ An arrow (▾) shows where the worksheet will appear.

■ The worksheet appears in the new location.

COLOR A WORKSHEET TAB

You can add color to a worksheet tab you want to stand out. This allows you to quickly locate a worksheet of interest.

Adding color to worksheet tabs can also help you organize a workbook that contains several worksheets. For example, you can add the same color to the tabs of worksheets that contain similar data.

COLOR A WORKSHEET TAB

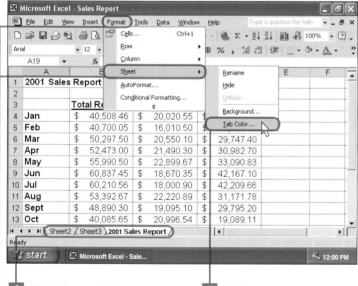

1 Click the worksheet tab you want to add color to.

2 Click **Format**.

3 Click **Sheet**.

4 Click **Tab Color**.

■ The Format Tab Color dialog box appears.

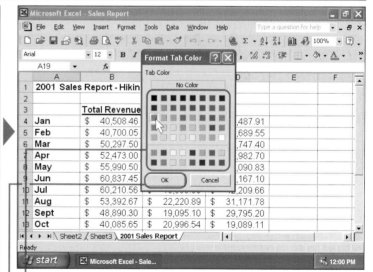

5 Click the color you want to use.

6 Click **OK**.

■ Excel adds the color you selected to the worksheet tab.

■ To remove color from a worksheet tab, repeat steps 1 to 6, selecting **No Color** in step 5.

You can move or copy data from one worksheet to another. This will save you time when you want to use data from another worksheet.

When you move data, the data disappears from its original location.

When you copy data, the data appears in both the original and new locations.

MOVE OR COPY DATA BETWEEN WORKSHEETS

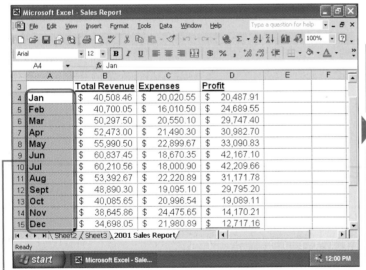

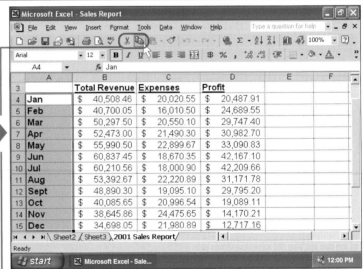

1 Select the cells containing the data you want to move or copy to another worksheet. To select cells, see page 12.

2 Click one of the following buttons.

✂ Move data

📋 Copy data

Note: If the button you want is not displayed, click ⟩ *on the Standard toolbar to display the button.*

■ The Clipboard task pane may appear, displaying items you have selected to move or copy. To use the Clipboard task pane, see the top of page 141.

140

How can I use the Clipboard task pane to move or copy data?

The Clipboard task pane displays up to the last 24 items you have selected to move or copy. To place a clipboard item into your worksheet, click the cell where you want to place the item and then click the item in the task pane. For more information on the task pane, see page 18.

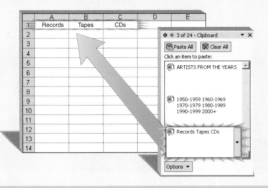

Why does the Paste Options button ( ) appear when I copy data?

You can use the Paste Options button ( ) to change the way Excel copies data. For example, you can specify that you want to use the column width from the original cells in the new location. Click the Paste Options button to display a list of options and then select the option you want to use. The Paste Options button is available only until you perform another task.

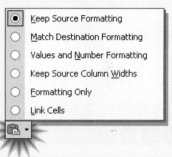

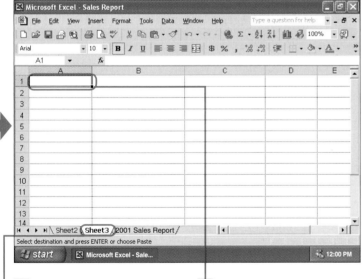

3 Click the tab for the worksheet where you want to place the data.

Note: To place the data in another workbook, open the workbook before performing step 3. To open a workbook, see page 30.

4 Click the cell where you want to place the data. This cell will become the top left cell of the new location.

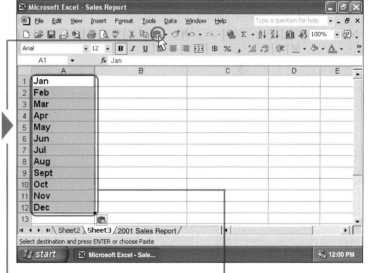

5 Click to place the data in the new location.

Note: If is not displayed, click on the Standard toolbar to display the button.

■ The data appears in the new location.

Note: If number signs (#) appear in a cell, the column is too narrow to fit the data. To change the column width, see page 48.

You can enter a formula that uses data from more than one worksheet.

If you change a number used in a formula you entered across worksheets, Excel will automatically redo the calculation for you. This ensures your calculations are always up to date.

ENTER A FORMULA ACROSS WORKSHEETS

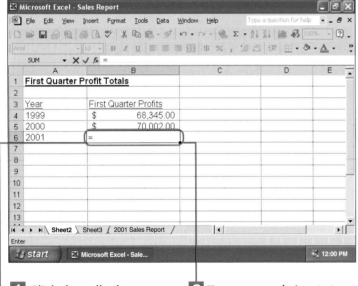

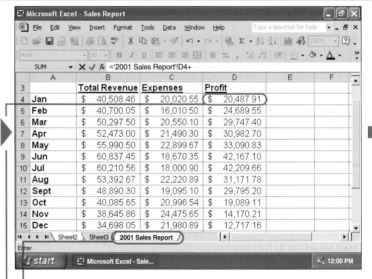

1 Click the cell where you want to enter a formula.

2 Type an equal sign (=) to begin the formula.

3 Click the tab for the worksheet containing the data you want to use in the formula.

4 Click a cell containing data you want to use in the formula.

5 Type the operator for the calculation you want to perform. For information on the types of operators you can use, see the top of page 143.

When entering a formula, what types of operators can I use?

Arithmetic operators allow you to perform mathematical calculations.

Arithmetic Operator:	Description:
+	Addition (A1 + B1)
-	Subtraction (A1-B1)
*	Multiplication (A1*B1)
/	Division (A1/B1)
%	Percent (A1%)
^	Exponentiation (A1 ^ B1)

Comparison operators allow you to compare two values. A formula that uses only a comparison operator will return a value of TRUE or FALSE.

Comparison Operator:	Description:
=	Equal to (A1 = B1)
>	Greater than (A1 > B1)
<	Less than (A1 < B1)
> =	Greater than or equal to (A1 > = B1)
< =	Less than or equal to (A1 < = B1)
< >	Not equal to (A1 < > B1)

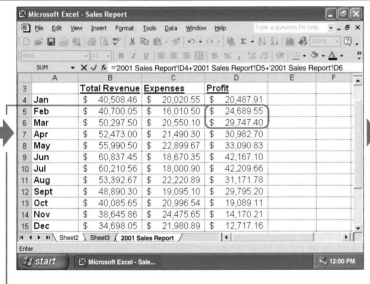

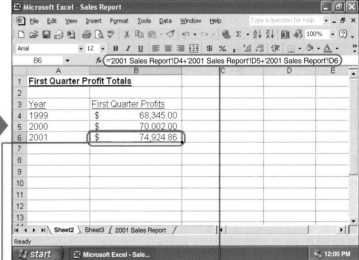

6 Repeat steps **3** to **5** until you have selected all the cells containing the data you want to use in the formula.

*Note: In this example, cells **D4** to **D6** are added together.*

7 Press the **Enter** key to complete the formula.

■ The result of the calculation appears in the cell you selected in step **1**.

8 To view the formula you entered, click the cell containing the formula.

■ The formula bar displays the worksheet name and cell reference for each cell used in the formula.

143

CHAPTER 9

WORK WITH CHARTS

Are you interested in displaying your worksheet data in a chart? In this chapter, you will learn how to create, change and print charts.

A chart allows you to visually display your worksheet data and can help you compare data and view trends. Excel offers many different chart types.

PARTS OF A CHART

Data Series

A group of related data representing one row or column from your worksheet. Each data series is represented by a specific color, pattern or symbol.

Chart Title

Identifies the subject of your chart.

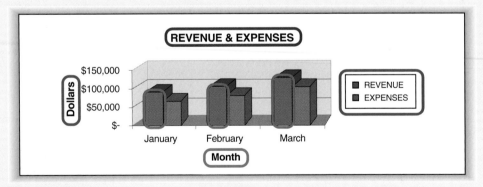

Legend

Identifies the color, pattern or symbol that represents each data series in your chart.

Value Axis Title

Indicates the unit of measure used in your chart.

Category Axis Title

Indicates the categories used in your chart.

COMMON CHART TYPES

Area

An area chart is useful for showing the amount of change in data over time. Each area represents a data series.

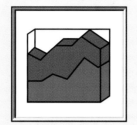

Line

A line chart is useful for showing changes to data at regular intervals. Each line represents a data series.

Column

A column chart is useful for showing changes to data over time or comparing individual items. Each column represents an item in a data series.

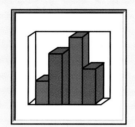

Bar

A bar chart is useful for comparing individual items. Each bar represents an item in a data series.

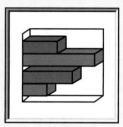

Pie

A pie chart is useful for showing the relationship of parts to a whole. Each piece of a pie represents an item in a data series. A pie chart can show only one data series at a time.

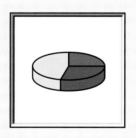

Doughnut

A doughnut chart is useful for showing the relationship of parts to a whole. Unlike a pie chart, a doughnut chart can display more than one data series. Each ring represents a data series.

Radar

A radar chart is useful for comparing the items in several data series. Each data series is shown as a line around a central point.

XY (Scatter)

An xy (scatter) chart is useful for showing the relationship between two or more data series measured at uneven intervals.

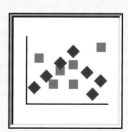

You can create a chart to graphically display your worksheet data. Charts allow you to easily compare data and view patterns and trends.

The Chart Wizard takes you step by step through the process of creating a chart.

CREATE A CHART

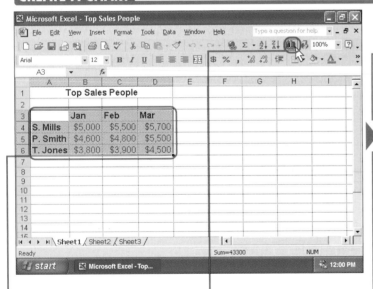

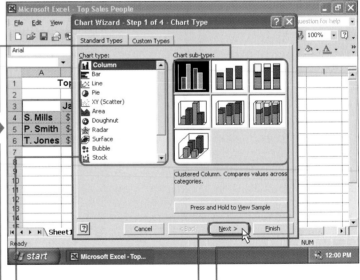

1 Select the cells containing the data you want to display in a chart, including the row and column labels. To select cells, see page 12.

2 Click 📊 to create a chart.

Note: If 📊 is not displayed, click 👉 on the Standard toolbar to display the button.

■ The Chart Wizard appears.

3 Click the type of chart you want to create.

■ This area displays the available chart designs for the type of chart you selected.

4 Click the chart design you want to use.

5 Click **Next** to continue.

SIMPLIFY IT

What titles can I add to my chart?

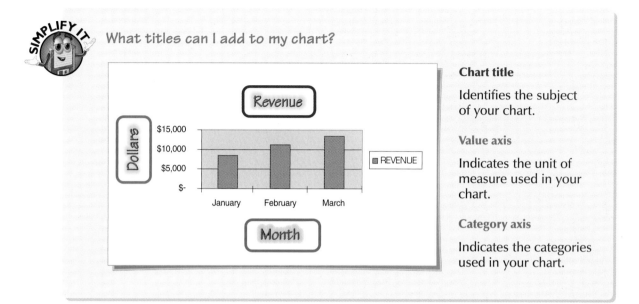

Chart title

Identifies the subject of your chart.

Value axis

Indicates the unit of measure used in your chart.

Category axis

Indicates the categories used in your chart.

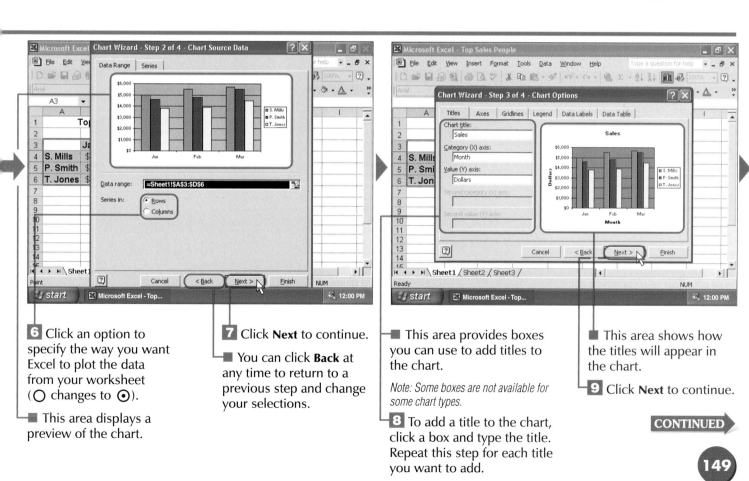

6 Click an option to specify the way you want Excel to plot the data from your worksheet (○ changes to ⊙).

■ This area displays a preview of the chart.

7 Click **Next** to continue.

■ You can click **Back** at any time to return to a previous step and change your selections.

■ This area provides boxes you can use to add titles to the chart.

Note: Some boxes are not available for some chart types.

8 To add a title to the chart, click a box and type the title. Repeat this step for each title you want to add.

■ This area shows how the titles will appear in the chart.

9 Click **Next** to continue.

CONTINUED

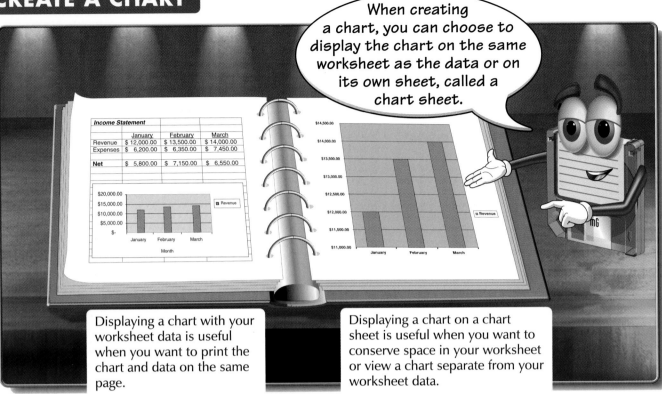

When creating a chart, you can choose to display the chart on the same worksheet as the data or on its own sheet, called a chart sheet.

Displaying a chart with your worksheet data is useful when you want to print the chart and data on the same page.

Displaying a chart on a chart sheet is useful when you want to conserve space in your worksheet or view a chart separate from your worksheet data.

CREATE A CHART (CONTINUED)

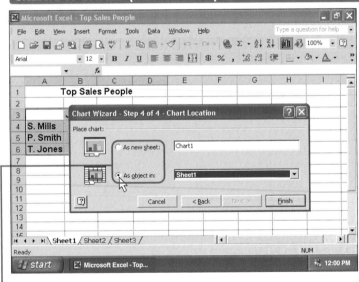

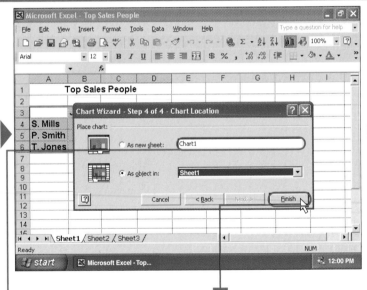

10 Click an option to specify where you want to display the chart (○ changes to ⊙).

As new sheet
Displays the chart on its own sheet, called a chart sheet.

As object in
Displays the chart on the same worksheet as the data.

■ If you selected **As new sheet** in step 10, you can type a name for the chart sheet in this area.

11 Click **Finish** to create the chart.

What happens if I change the data I used to create a chart?

If you change the data you used to create a chart, Excel will automatically update the chart to display the changes.

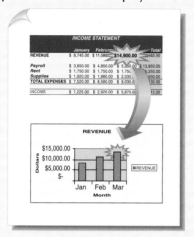

Is there a way to quickly create a chart?

To quickly create a basic chart, select the cells containing the data you want to display in the chart and then press the F11 key. The chart will appear on its own chart sheet.

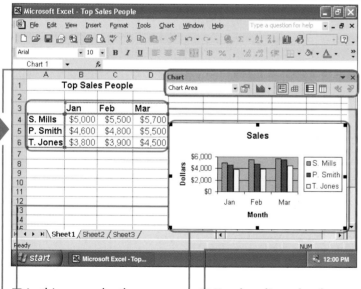

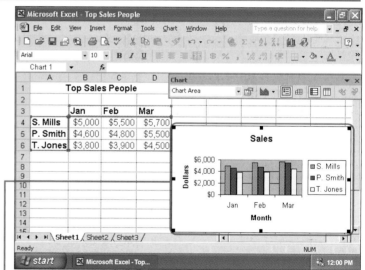

■ In this example, the chart appears on the same worksheet as the data.

■ The Chart toolbar also appears, displaying buttons that allow you to make changes to the chart.

■ Excel outlines the data you selected to create the chart.

■ The handles (■) around a chart allow you to change the size of the chart. To hide the handles, click outside the chart.

Note: To move or resize a chart, see page 152.

DELETE A CHART

1 Click a blank area in the chart you want to delete. Handles (■) appear around the chart.

2 Press the Delete key to delete the chart.

Note: To delete a chart displayed on a chart sheet, you must delete the sheet. To delete a worksheet, see page 137.

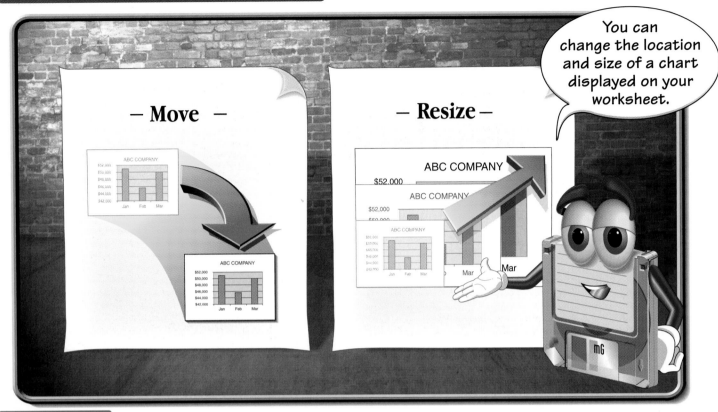

— Move —

— Resize —

You can change the location and size of a chart displayed on your worksheet.

MOVE A CHART

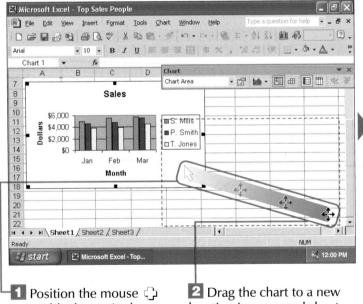

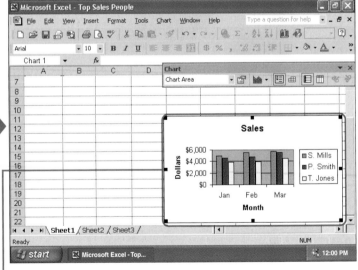

1 Position the mouse ⬚ over a blank area in the chart you want to move (⬚ changes to ⬚).

2 Drag the chart to a new location in your worksheet.

■ A dashed line indicates where the chart will appear.

■ The chart appears in the new location.

■ To deselect the chart, click outside the chart.

What handle (■) should I use to resize a chart?

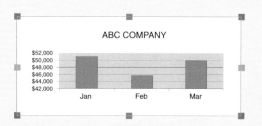

- Changes the height of a chart.
- Changes the width of a chart.
- Changes the height and width of a chart at the same time.

Can I move individual items in a chart?

Yes. To move the chart title, an axis title or the legend to a new location in a chart, position the mouse � over the item. Then drag the item to a new location. You cannot move an item outside of the chart area.

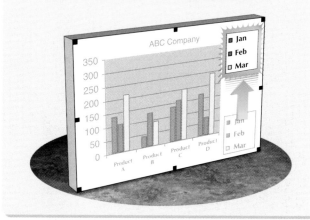

RESIZE A CHART

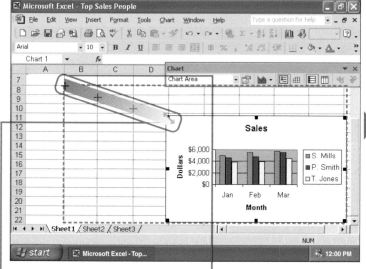

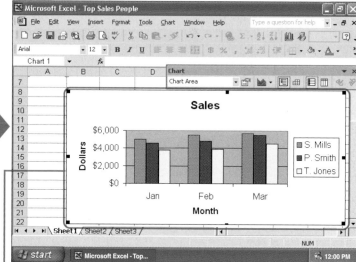

1 Click a blank area in the chart you want to resize. Handles (■) appear around the chart.

2 Position the mouse � over one of the handles (� changes to ↘, ↗, ↔ or ↕).

3 Drag the handle until the chart is the size you want.

■ A dashed line shows the new size.

■ The chart appears in the new size.

■ To deselect the chart, click outside the chart.

153

PRINT A CHART

You can print a chart with the worksheet data or on its own page.

Print a chart with worksheet data

Print a chart on its own page

When you print a chart on its own page, the chart will expand to fill the page.

PRINT A CHART

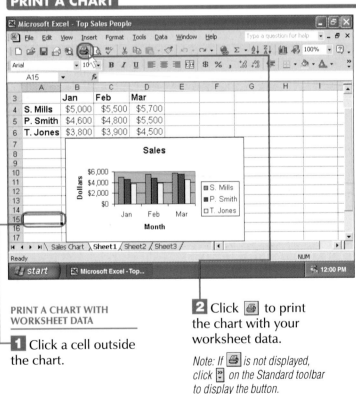

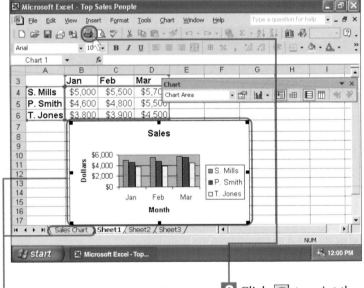

PRINT A CHART WITH WORKSHEET DATA

1 Click a cell outside the chart.

2 Click 🖨 to print the chart with your worksheet data.

Note: If 🖨 is not displayed, click 🔽 on the Standard toolbar to display the button.

PRINT A CHART ON ITS OWN PAGE

1 To print a chart displayed on a worksheet, click a blank area in the chart.

■ To print a chart displayed on a chart sheet, click the tab for the chart sheet.

2 Click 🖨 to print the chart on its own page.

Note: If 🖨 is not displayed, click 🔽 on the Standard toolbar to display the button.

154

After you create a chart, you can change the chart type to present your data more effectively.

The type of chart you should use depends on your data. For example, area, column and line charts are ideal for showing changes to values over time. Pie charts are ideal for showing percentages.

CHANGE THE CHART TYPE

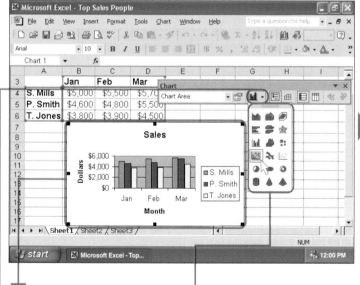

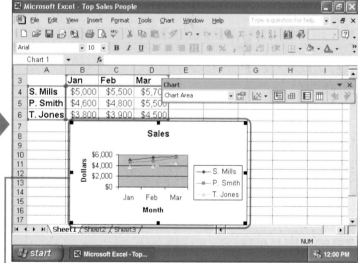

1 Click a blank area in the chart you want to change. Handles (■) appear around the chart.

2 Click ⬚ in this area to display the available chart types.

Note: If the Chart toolbar is not displayed, see page 82 to display the toolbar.

3 Click the type of chart you want to use.

■ The chart displays the chart type you selected.

■ To deselect the chart, click outside the chart.

155

CHANGE CHART TITLES

You can change the chart and axis titles in a chart to make the titles more meaningful.

CHANGE CHART TITLES

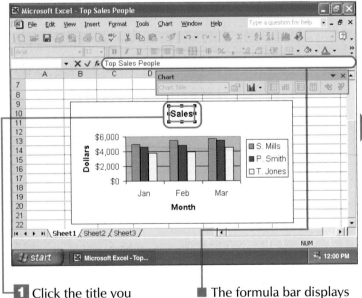

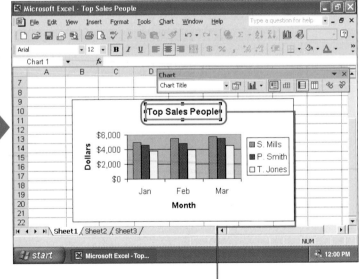

1 Click the title you want to change. A box appears around the title.

2 Type the new title.

■ The formula bar displays the title as you type.

3 Press the Enter key to add the title to the chart.

■ The chart displays the new title.

■ To deselect the title, click outside the chart.

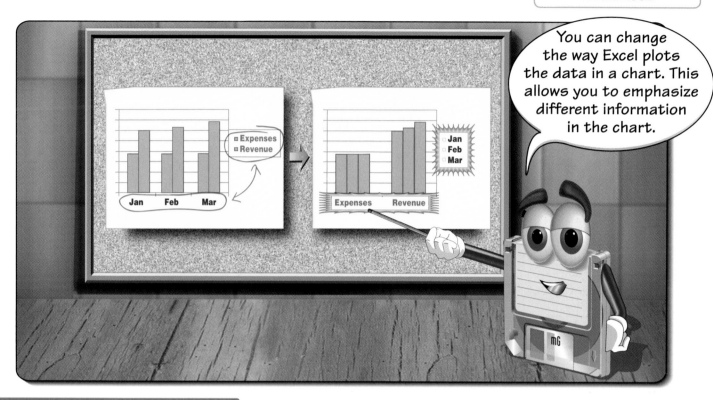

You can change the way Excel plots the data in a chart. This allows you to emphasize different information in the chart.

CHANGE THE WAY DATA IS PLOTTED

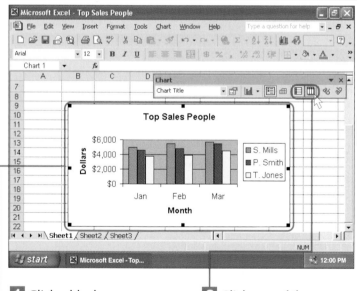

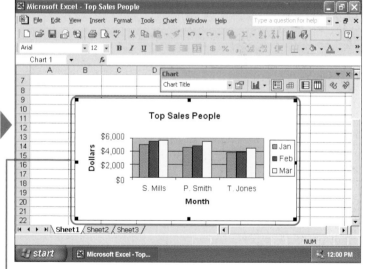

1 Click a blank area in the chart you want to change. Handles (■) appear around the chart.

2 Click one of the following buttons.

▦ Plot data by row

▦ Plot data by column

Note: If the Chart toolbar is not displayed, see page 82 to display the toolbar.

■ The chart displays the change.

■ To deselect the chart, click outside the chart.

After you create a chart, you can add new data to the chart.

Adding data to a chart is useful when you need to update the chart. For example, you can add the latest sales figures to your chart at the end of each month.

ADD DATA TO A CHART

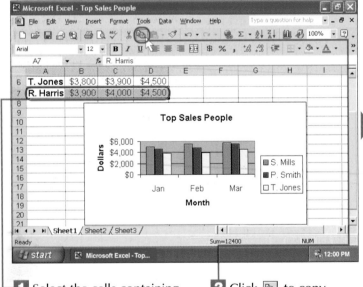

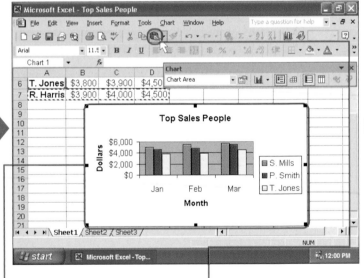

1 Select the cells containing the data you want to add to the chart, including the row or column labels. To select cells, see page 12.

2 Click 📋 to copy the data.

Note: If 📋 is not displayed, click ⟫ on the Standard toolbar to display the button.

3 Click the chart you want to add the data to.

4 Click 📋 to add the data to the chart.

Note: If 📋 is not displayed, click ⟫ on the Standard toolbar to display the button.

Can I add a data series to a pie chart?

A pie chart can display only one data series. You cannot add another data series to a pie chart.

Jan Sales

Feb Sales

How can I add a data series to a chart displayed on a chart sheet?

To add a data series to a chart displayed on a chart sheet, perform steps 1 and 2 on page 158. Click the tab for the chart sheet containing the chart you want to add the data series to and then perform step 4.

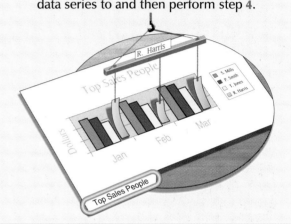

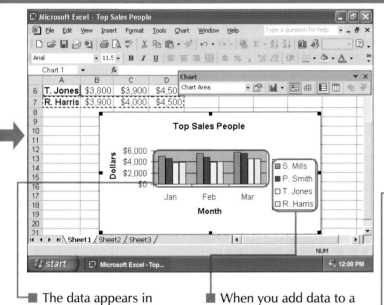

■ The data appears in the chart.

■ When you add data to a chart, Excel automatically updates the chart legend.

DELETE DATA FROM A CHART

1 Click the data you want to remove from the chart. Handles (■) appear on the data series.

2 Press the Delete key to delete the data from the chart.

159

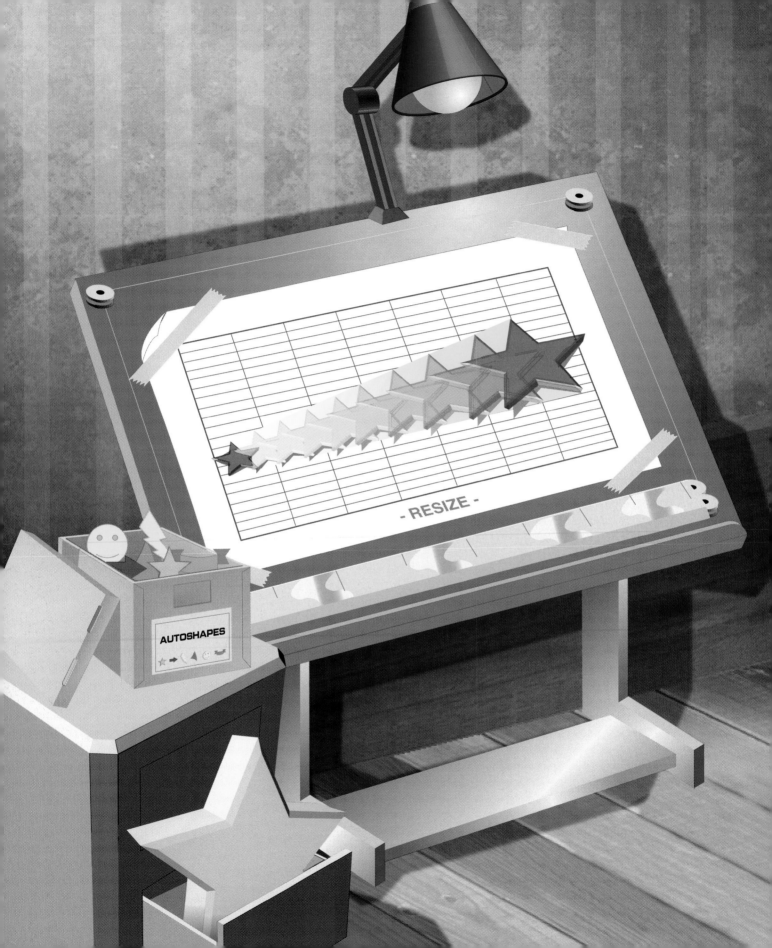

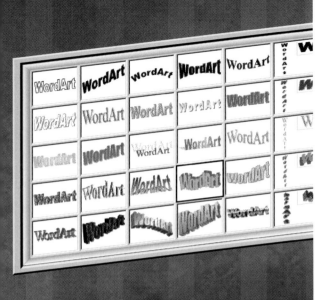

CHAPTER 10

WORK WITH OBJECTS

Are you wondering how to use objects, such as AutoShapes and clip art images, to enhance the appearance of your worksheet? This chapter shows you how.

Hockey Stats

	Wins	Losses	Ties	
Cougars	25	21	4	2
Greyhounds	13	13	2	1
Pirates	37	37	2	2
Bears	20	20	2	10
Cardinals	26	26		
Red Hawks	30	30		

You can add WordArt to your worksheet or chart to create an eye-catching title or draw attention to important information.

ADD WORDART

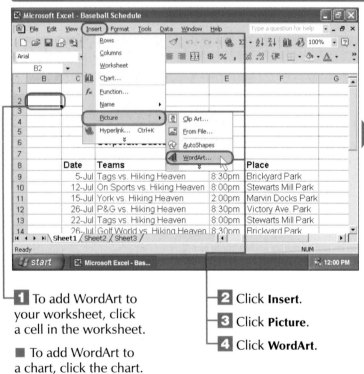

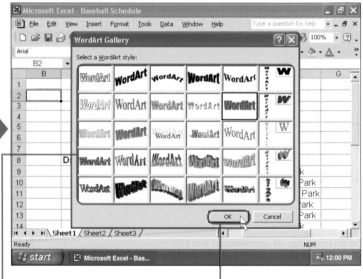

1 To add WordArt to your worksheet, click a cell in the worksheet.

■ To add WordArt to a chart, click the chart.

2 Click **Insert**.

3 Click **Picture**.

4 Click **WordArt**.

■ The WordArt Gallery dialog box appears.

5 Click the WordArt style you want to use.

6 Click **OK** to confirm your selection.

162

How do I edit WordArt text?

To edit WordArt text, double-click the WordArt to display the Edit WordArt Text dialog box. Then perform steps **7** and **8** below to specify the new text you want the WordArt to display.

Why does the WordArt toolbar appear when I add WordArt to a worksheet or chart?

The WordArt toolbar contains buttons that allow you to change the appearance of WordArt. For example, you can click one of the following buttons to alter the appearance of WordArt.

Aa Display all the letters in the WordArt at the same height.

b̃ Display the WordArt text vertically rather than horizontally.

■ The Edit WordArt Text dialog box appears.

7 Type the text you want the WordArt to display.

8 Click **OK** to add the WordArt to your worksheet or chart.

■ The WordArt appears. The handles (o) around the WordArt allow you to change the size of the WordArt. To move or resize WordArt, see page 172 or 173.

■ To deselect WordArt, click outside the WordArt.

DELETE WORDART

1 Click the WordArt you want to delete. Handles (o) appear around the WordArt.

2 Press the Delete key to delete the WordArt.

163

Excel offers several types of AutoShapes such as lines, arrows, stars and banners.

ADD AN AUTOSHAPE

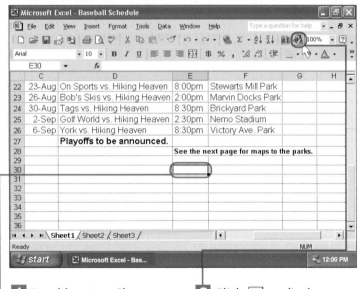

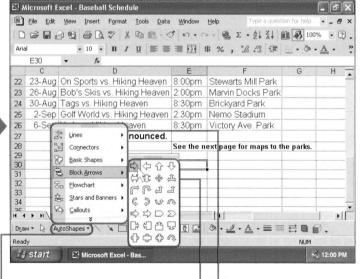

1 To add an AutoShape to your worksheet, click a cell in the worksheet.

■ To add an AutoShape to a chart, click the chart.

2 Click 🔲 to display the Drawing toolbar.

Note: If 🔲 is not displayed, click ⁇ on the Standard toolbar to display the button.

■ The Drawing toolbar appears.

3 Click **AutoShapes**.

4 Click the type of AutoShape you want to add.

5 Click the AutoShape you want to add.

Can I add text to an AutoShape?

You can add text to most AutoShapes. This is particularly useful for AutoShapes such as banners and callouts. To add text to an AutoShape, click the AutoShape and then type the text you want the AutoShape to display.

CONGRATULATIONS!

How do I delete an AutoShape?

To delete an AutoShape, click an edge of the AutoShape and then press the Delete key.

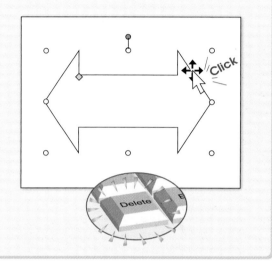

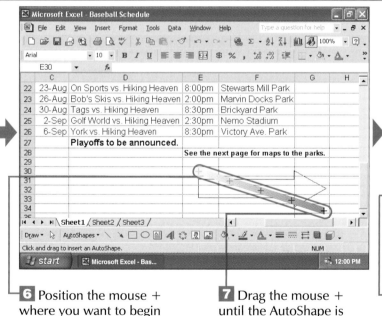

6 Position the mouse + where you want to begin drawing the AutoShape.

7 Drag the mouse + until the AutoShape is the size you want.

■ The AutoShape appears. The handles (○) around the AutoShape allow you to change the size of the AutoShape. To move or resize an AutoShape, see page 172 or 173.

■ To deselect an AutoShape, click outside the AutoShape.

Note: To hide the Drawing toolbar, repeat step 2.

ADD A TEXT BOX

You can add a text box to your worksheet or chart to display additional information.

Text boxes are useful for displaying notes. You can also use text boxes to label or describe items in your worksheet or chart.

ADD A TEXT BOX

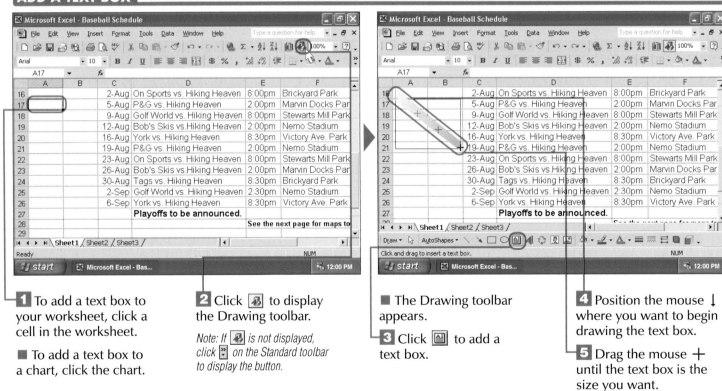

1 To add a text box to your worksheet, click a cell in the worksheet.

■ To add a text box to a chart, click the chart.

2 Click 🖾 to display the Drawing toolbar.

Note: If 🖾 is not displayed, click 🔽 on the Standard toolbar to display the button.

■ The Drawing toolbar appears.

3 Click 🖾 to add a text box.

4 Position the mouse ↓ where you want to begin drawing the text box.

5 Drag the mouse ✛ until the text box is the size you want.

166

How do I edit the text in a text box?

To edit the text in a text box, click the text box and then edit the text as you would edit any text in your worksheet. When you finish editing the text, click outside the text box.

Can I format the text in a text box?

Yes. Click the text box and then drag the mouse I over the text you want to format until you highlight the text. You can then format the text as you would format any text in your worksheet. For example, you can change the font and size of text or bold, italicize and underline text. To format text, see pages 90 to 96.

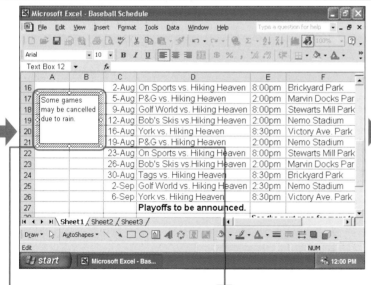

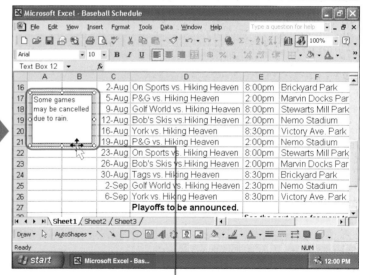

■ The text box appears. The handles (○) around the text box allow you to change the size of the text box. To move or resize a text box, see page 172 or 173.

6 Type the text you want the text box to display.

■ To deselect a text box, click outside the text box.

Note: To hide the Drawing toolbar, repeat step 2.

DELETE A TEXT BOX

1 Click an edge of the text box you want to delete. Handles (○) appear around the text box.

2 Press the Delete key to delete the text box.

ADD A CLIP ART IMAGE

You can add professionally-designed clip art images to your worksheet or chart. Clip art images can help illustrate concepts and make your worksheet or chart more interesting.

ADD A CLIP ART IMAGE

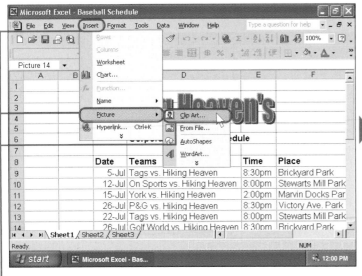

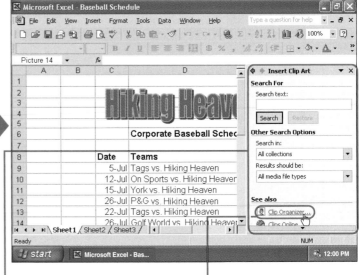

1 Click **Insert**.

2 Click **Picture**.

3 Click **Clip Art**.

*Note: The first time you add a clip art image to a worksheet or chart, the Add Clips to Organizer dialog box appears. Click **Now** in the dialog box to catalog the image, sound and video files on your computer.*

■ The Insert Clip Art task pane appears.

4 Click **Clip Organizer** to view the image, sound and video files in the Clip Organizer.

■ The Microsoft Clip Organizer window appears.

How does the Clip Organizer arrange image, sound and video files?

The Clip Organizer arranges media files into three main folders.

My Collections

Displays the media files you have specified as your favorites and media files that came with Microsoft Windows.

Office Collections

Displays the media files that came with Microsoft Office.

Web Collections

Displays the media files that are available at Microsoft's Web site and Web sites in partnership with Microsoft.

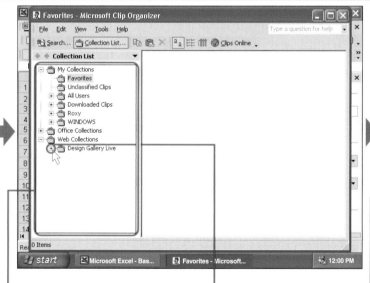

■ This area lists the folders that contain image, sound and video files that you can add to your worksheet.

■ A folder displaying a plus sign (⊞) contains hidden folders.

5 To display the hidden folders within a folder, click a plus sign (⊞) beside a folder (⊞ changes to ⊟).

Note: You must be connected to the Internet to view the contents of the Web Collections folder.

■ The hidden folders appear.

Note: To once again hide the folders within a folder, click a minus sign (⊟) beside a folder.

6 Click a folder of interest.

■ This area displays the contents of the folder you selected.

7 Click the image you want to add to your worksheet or chart.

CONTINUED ▶

ADD A CLIP ART IMAGE

After you locate an image you want to add to your worksheet or chart, you can copy the image and then place the image in your worksheet or chart.

ADD A CLIP ART IMAGE (CONTINUED)

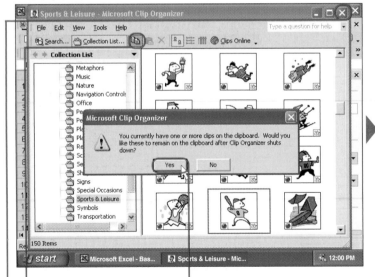

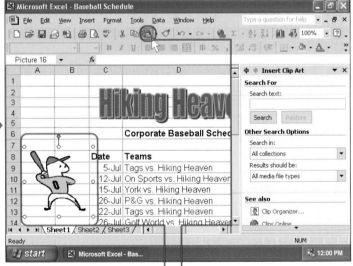

8 Click 📋 to copy the image you selected.

9 Click ✕ to close the Microsoft Clip Organizer window.

■ A dialog box appears, stating that you have one or more clip art images on the clipboard.

Note: The clipboard temporarily stores information you have selected to move or copy.

10 Click **Yes** to keep the image on the clipboard.

11 To add the image to your worksheet, click a cell in the worksheet.

■ To add the image to a chart, click the chart.

12 Click 📋 to place the image in your worksheet or chart.

■ The clip art image appears. The handles (o) around the clip art image allow you to change the size of the image. To move or resize an image, see page 172 or 173.

Where can I obtain more clip art images?

You can buy collections of clip art images at computer stores. Many Web sites, such as www.allfree-clipart.com and www.noeticart.com, also offer clip art images you can use in your worksheet or chart.

How do I delete a clip art image?

To delete a clip art image, click the clip art image and then press the Delete key.

SEARCH FOR A CLIP ART IMAGE

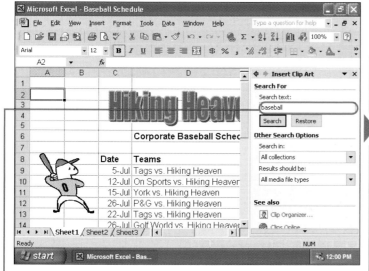

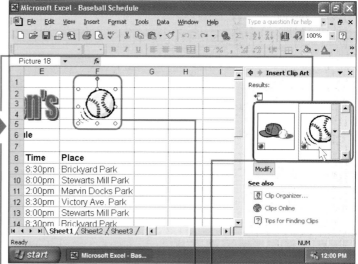

You can search for clip art images by specifying one or more words of interest.

1 Click this area and then type one or more words that describe the clip art image you want to find. Then press the Enter key.

Note: If the Insert Clip Art task pane is not displayed, perform steps 1 to 3 on page 168 to display the task pane.

■ This area displays the images that match the words you specified.

2 To add an image to your worksheet, click a cell in the worksheet.

■ To add an image to a chart, click the chart.

3 Click the image you want to add to your worksheet or chart.

■ The image appears in your worksheet or chart.

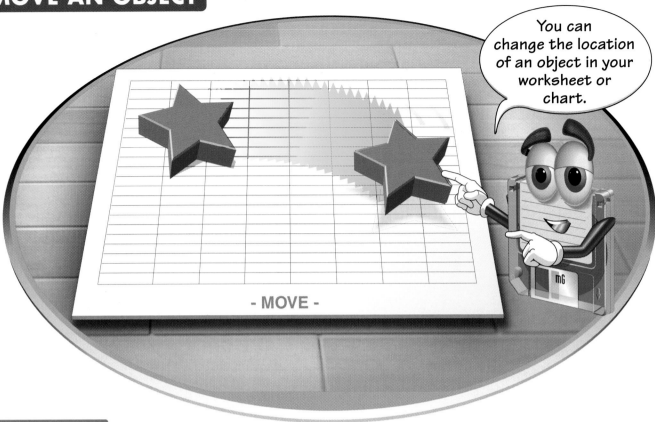

You can change the location of an object in your worksheet or chart.

- MOVE -

MOVE AN OBJECT

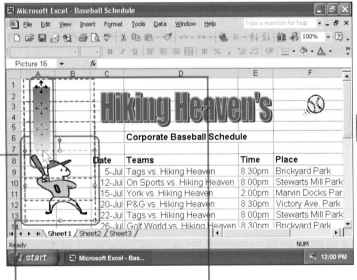

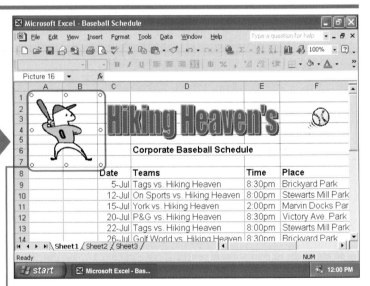

1 Click the object you want to move. Handles (o) appear around the object.

2 Position the mouse ⇩ over an edge of the object (⇩ changes to ✛).

3 Drag the object to a new location.

■ A dashed line indicates where the object will appear.

■ The object appears in the new location.

Note: If you added an object to a chart, you cannot move the object outside the chart area.

■ To deselect the object, click outside the object.

You can change the size of an object in your worksheet or chart.

- RESIZE -

RESIZE AN OBJECT

1 Click the object you want to resize. Handles (o) appear around the object.

2 Position the mouse ⊕ over one of the handles (⊕ changes to ↗, ↘, ↔ or ↕).

3 Drag the handle until the object is the size you want.

■ A dashed line indicates the new size.

■ The object appears in the new size.

■ To deselect the object, click outside the object.

CHANGE COLOR OF AN OBJECT

You can change the color of an object in your worksheet or chart.

You cannot change the color of some clip art images and pictures.

CHANGE COLOR OF AN OBJECT

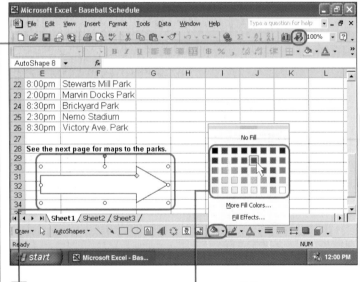

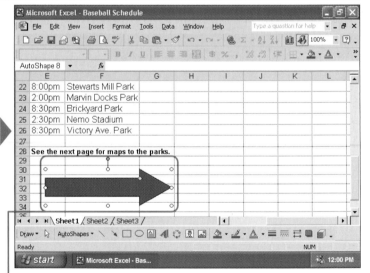

1 Click an edge of the object you want to change to a different color. Handles (o) appear around the object.

2 Click ![icon] to display the Drawing toolbar.

Note: If ![icon] is not displayed, click ![icon] on the Standard toolbar to display the button.

3 Click ![icon] in this area to display the available colors.

4 Click the color you want to use.

■ The object appears in the color you selected.

■ To deselect an object, click outside the object.

Note: To hide the Drawing toolbar, repeat step 2.

174

ROTATE AN OBJECT

You cannot rotate text boxes and some AutoShapes.

ROTATE AN OBJECT

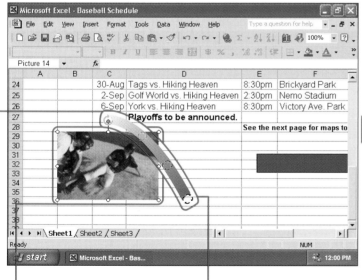

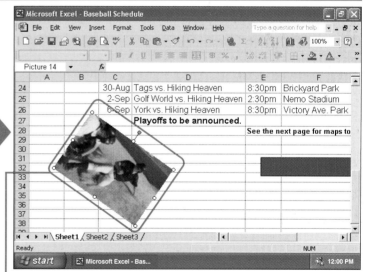

1 Click the object you want to rotate. Handles (o) appear around the object.

2 Position the mouse ⊕ over the green dot (⊕ changes to ↻).

3 Drag the mouse ↻ in the direction you want to rotate the object.

■ The object appears in the new position.

■ To deselect an object, click outside the object.

175

You can add a diagram to a worksheet to illustrate a concept or idea. Excel provides several types of diagrams for you to choose from.

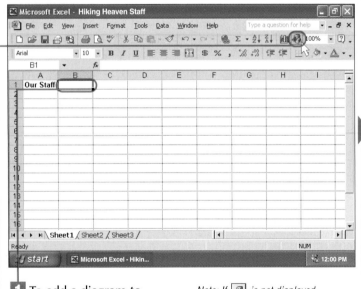

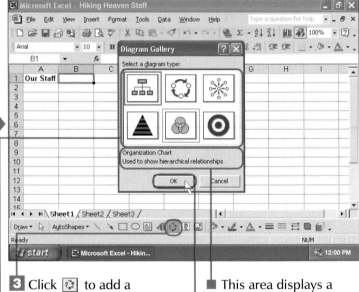

1 To add a diagram to your worksheet, click a cell in the worksheet.

2 Click 📊 to display the Drawing toolbar.

Note: If 📊 is not displayed, click ⏵⏵ on the Standard toolbar to display the button.

■ The Drawing toolbar appears.

3 Click 🔄 to add a diagram to your worksheet.

■ The Diagram Gallery dialog box appears.

4 Click the type of diagram you want to add.

■ This area displays a description of the diagram you selected.

5 Click **OK** to add the diagram to your worksheet.

SIMPLIFY IT

What types of diagrams can I add to my worksheet?

Organization Chart
Shows how items are related and ranked.

Cycle
Shows a procedure that has an uninterrupted cycle.

Radial
Shows how items relate to a central item.

Pyramid
Shows how items build on one another.

Venn
Shows areas of similarity between items.

Target
Shows a progression towards a goal.

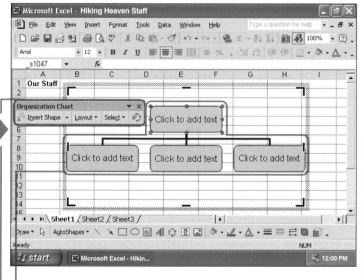

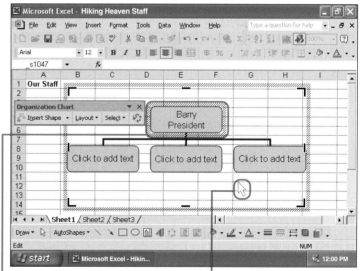

■ The diagram appears in your worksheet.

■ A toolbar also appears, displaying buttons that allow you to change the diagram.

■ To deselect a diagram, click outside the diagram.

Note: To hide the Drawing toolbar, repeat step 2.

ADD TEXT

1 Click an area where you want to add text.

■ A border appears around the area if you can add text to the area.

2 Type the text you want to add.

3 When you finish typing the text, click outside the text area.

■ Repeat steps 1 to 3 for each area of text you want to add.

CONTINUED ➤

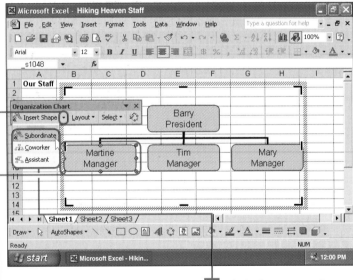

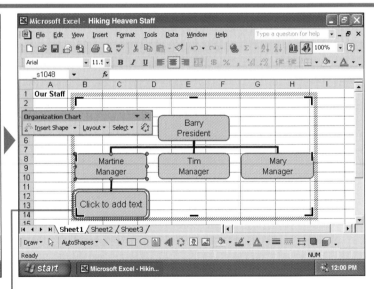

ADD A SHAPE

1 Click the shape above or beside where you want the new shape to appear.

2 To add a shape to an organization chart, click ⊡ beside **Insert Shape**.

3 Click the option that describes where you want to position the shape.

Note: For information on the available positions, see the top of page 179.

■ To add a shape to all other types of diagrams, click **Insert Shape**.

■ The new shape appears in the diagram.

■ You can add text to the new shape.

■ To delete a shape, click an edge of the shape you want to delete and then press the Delete key.

Where can I position a shape I add to an organization chart?

Subordinate
Adds a shape below the shape you selected.

Coworker
Adds a shape beside the shape you selected.

Assistant
Uses an elbow connector to add a shape below the shape you selected.

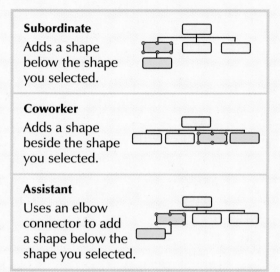

How do I delete a diagram?

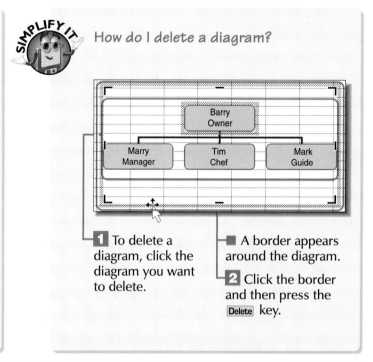

1 To delete a diagram, click the diagram you want to delete.

■ A border appears around the diagram.

2 Click the border and then press the Delete key.

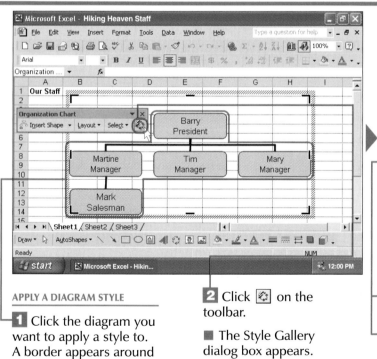

APPLY A DIAGRAM STYLE

1 Click the diagram you want to apply a style to. A border appears around the diagram.

2 Click 🖫 on the toolbar.

■ The Style Gallery dialog box appears.

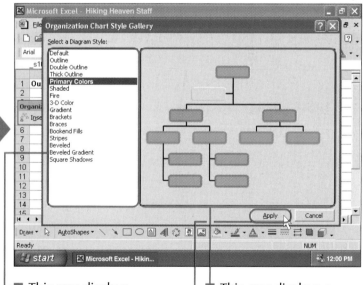

■ This area displays the available styles.

3 Click the style you want to use.

■ This area displays a preview of the style you selected.

4 Click **Apply** to apply the style to the diagram.

■ To remove a diagram style, repeat steps **1** to **4**, selecting **Default** in step **3**.

LAST NAME	FIRST NAME	PRODUCT	UNITS SOLD
Marcuson	Jason	A	632
Matthews	Kathleen	A	1625
Petterson	Brenda	A	685
Robinson	Melanie	A	812
Smith	Jill	B	956
Smith	Linda	B	701
Toppins	Allen	B	598
		B Subtotal	**2255**
Dean	Chuck	C	934
Martin	Jim	C	795
		C Subtotal	**1729**

A Subtotal   3754

CHAPTER 11

MANAGE DATA IN A LIST

Would you like Excel to help you organize a large collection of data? In this chapter, you will learn how to sort data in a list, add subtotals to a list and more.

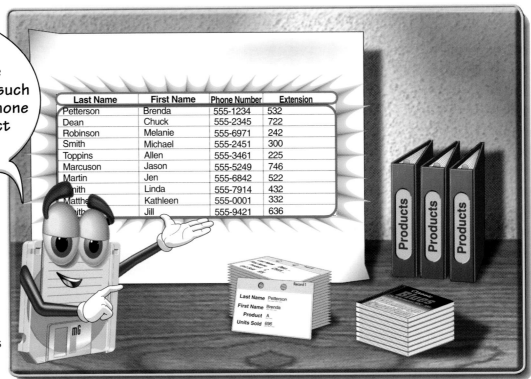

You can create a list to organize a large collection of data, such as a mailing list, phone directory, product list or music collection.

The first row in a list contains the column labels for the list. A **column label** describes the data in a column. Each row in a list contains one record. A **record** is a group of related data.

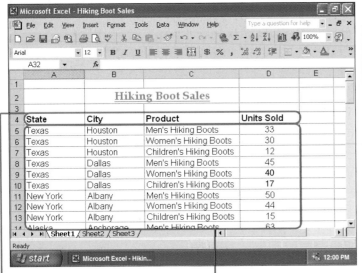

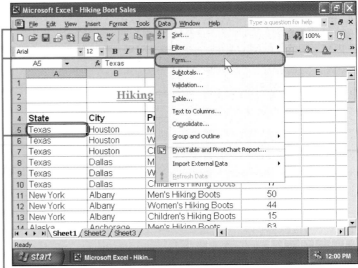

1 Type the column labels that describe the data you will enter into each column.

■ In this example, we bold the column labels to ensure that Excel will recognize the text as column labels. To bold text, see page 92.

2 Enter the data for each record.

Note: For guidelines on creating a list, see the top of page 183.

ADD RECORDS USING A DATA FORM

1 Click a cell in the list.

2 Click **Data**.

3 Click **Form**.

Note: If Form does not appear on the menu, position the mouse over the bottom of the menu to display all the menu options.

182

What should I consider when creating a list?

➢ Create only one list on a worksheet.

➢ Do not include blank rows or columns in the list.

➢ Keep the list separate from other data on the worksheet. For example, leave a blank row or column between the list and other data.

➢ Format the column labels to ensure that Excel will recognize the text as column labels. To format text, see pages 90 to 97.

➢ When entering data into a cell in the list, do not enter blank spaces at the beginning or end of the data.

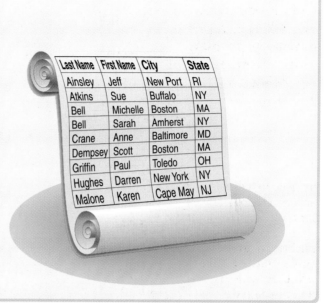

Last Name	First Name	City	State
Ainsley	Jeff	New Port	RI
Atkins	Sue	Buffalo	NY
Bell	Michelle	Boston	MA
Bell	Sarah	Amherst	NY
Crane	Anne	Baltimore	MD
Dempsey	Scott	Boston	MA
Griffin	Paul	Toledo	OH
Hughes	Darren	New York	NY
Malone	Karen	Cape May	NJ

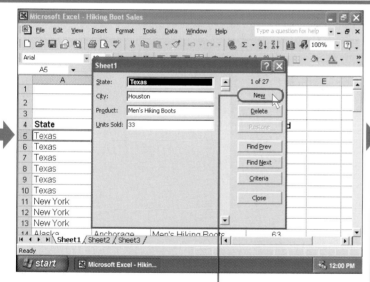

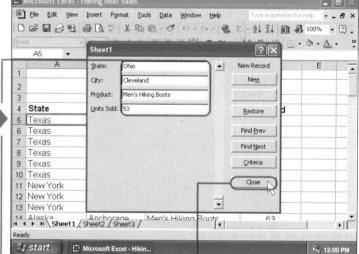

■ A data form dialog box appears, displaying the data for the first record in the list.

4 Click **New** to add a new record to the list.

5 Type the data that corresponds to the first column label and then press the Tab key. Repeat this step until you have entered all the data for the record.

6 Repeat steps 4 and 5 for each record you want to add.

7 Click **Close** when you have finished entering records.

You can search for records in your list that contain specific data.

For example, you can have Excel find all the records for stores located in California.

FIND DATA IN A LIST

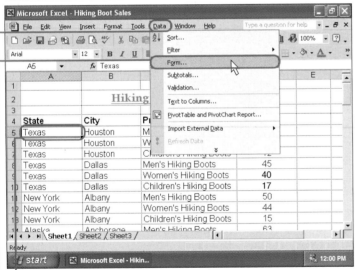

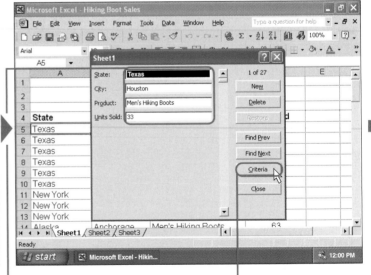

1 Click a cell in the list.

2 Click **Data**.

3 Click **Form**.

Note: If Form does not appear on the menu, position the mouse over the bottom of the menu to display all the menu options.

■ A data form dialog box appears, displaying the data for the first record in the list.

4 Click **Criteria** to specify the data you want to search for.

What operators can I use to find specific data in my list?

Operator:	Example:	Result:
=	=100	Finds the number 100.
	=California	Finds California.
>	>100	Finds numbers greater than 100.
	>N	Finds text starting with the letters N to Z.
<	<100	Finds numbers less than 100.
	<N	Finds text starting with the letters A to M.
>=	>=100	Finds numbers greater than or equal to 100.
	>=N	Finds the letter N and text starting with the letters N to Z.
<=	<=100	Finds numbers less than or equal to 100.
	<=N	Finds the letter N and text starting with the letters A to M.
<>	<>100	Finds numbers not equal to 100.
	<>California	Finds text not equal to California.

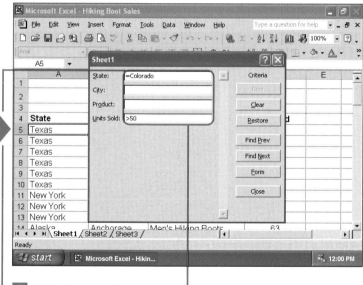

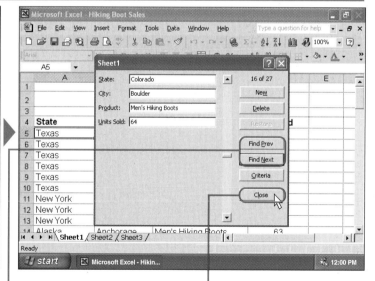

5 Click the area that corresponds to the column you want to use to find data.

6 Type an operator for the search and then type the data you want to find.

Note: For information on operators, see the top of this page.

7 Repeat steps 5 and 6 for each column you want to use to find data.

8 Click one of the following options.

Find Prev - Display previous matching record.

Find Next - Display next matching record.

9 Repeat step 8 until you finish viewing all the matching records.

10 Click **Close** to close the data form dialog box.

SORT BY ONE COLUMN

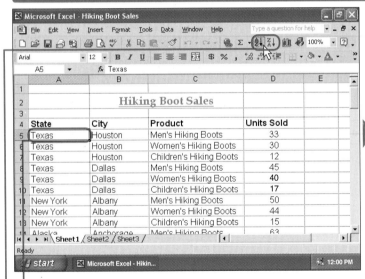

1 Click a cell in the column you want to sort by.

2 Click one of the following buttons.

- Sort 0 to 9, A to Z
- Sort 9 to 0, Z to A

Note: If the button you want is not displayed, click ⟫ *on the Standard toolbar to display the button.*

■ The records in the list appear in the new order.

■ In this example, the records are sorted by state.

■ To immediately reverse the results of sorting records, click ↶.

Note: If ↶ *is not displayed, click* ⟫ *on the Standard toolbar to display the button.*

Why would I sort my list by more than one column?

Sorting by more than one column allows you to further organize the data in your list. For example, if a last name appears more than once in the Last Name column, you can sort by a second column, such as the First Name column.

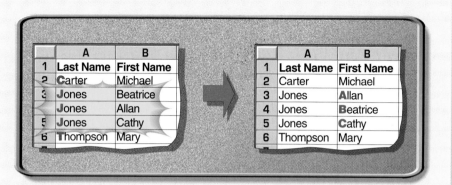

	A	B
1	**Last Name**	**First Name**
2	Carter	Michael
3	Jones	Beatrice
4	Jones	Allan
5	Jones	Cathy
6	Thompson	Mary

	A	B
1	**Last Name**	**First Name**
2	Carter	Michael
3	Jones	Allan
4	Jones	Beatrice
5	Jones	Cathy
6	Thompson	Mary

SORT BY TWO COLUMNS

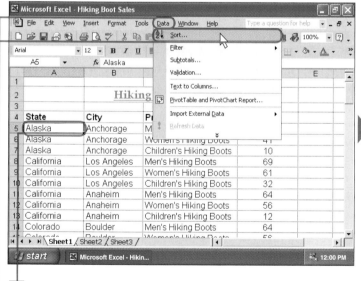

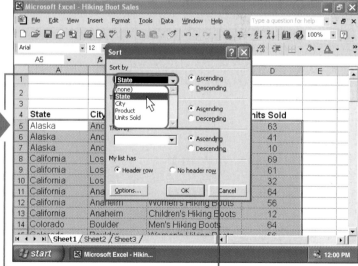

1 Click a cell in the list.

2 Click **Data**.

3 Click **Sort**.

■ The Sort dialog box appears.

4 Click ▼ in this area to select the first column you want to sort by.

5 Click the name of the first column you want to sort by.

CONTINUED ➤

187

SORT BY TWO COLUMNS (CONTINUED)

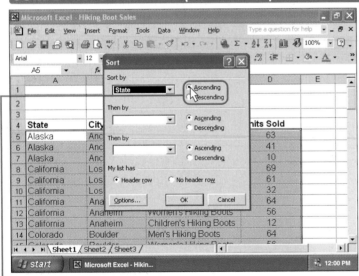

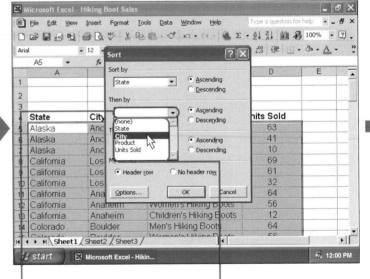

6 Click an option to specify the way you want to sort the first column (○ changes to ⦿).

Ascending
Sort 0 to 9, A to Z

Descending
Sort 9 to 0, Z to A

7 Click ▼ in this area to select the second column you want to sort by.

8 Click the name of the column you want to sort by.

SIMPLIFY IT

How often can I sort the records in my list?

You can sort the records in your list as often as you like. Sorting is useful if you frequently add new records to your list.

SIMPLIFY IT

How will Excel sort records if I sort by a column that contains blank cells?

If you sort by a column that contains blank cells, Excel will place the records containing the blank cells at the end of your list.

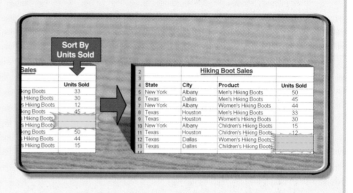

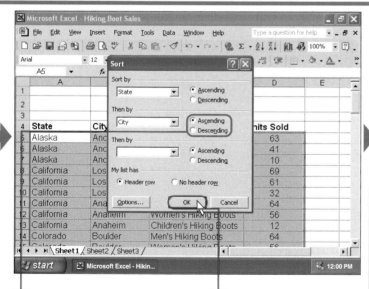

9 Click an option to specify the way you want to sort the second column (○ changes to ⊙).

10 Click **OK** to sort the records.

■ The records in the list appear in the new order.

■ In this example, the records are sorted by state. When a state appears more than once in the list, the records are then sorted by city.

■ To immediately reverse the results of sorting records, click ↺.

Note: If ↺ is not displayed, click » on the Standard toolbar to display the button.

FILTER A LIST

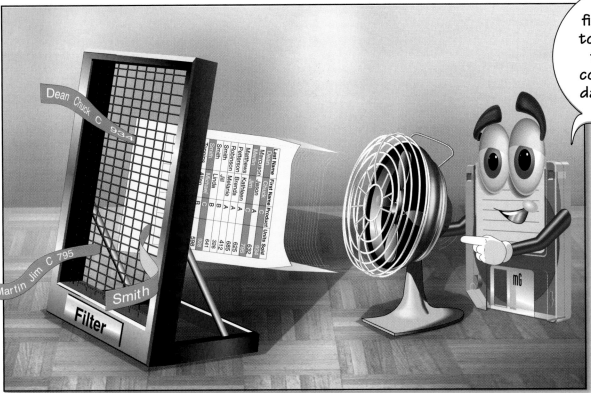

You can filter your list to display only the records containing the data you want to review.

The AutoFilter feature allows you to analyze your data by placing related records together and hiding the records you do not want to review.

FILTER A LIST

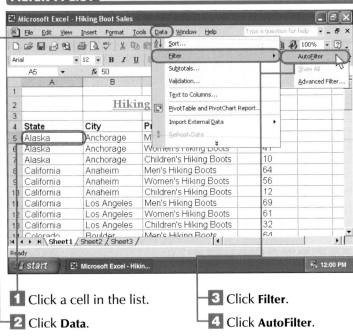

1 Click a cell in the list.

2 Click **Data**.

3 Click **Filter**.

4 Click **AutoFilter**.

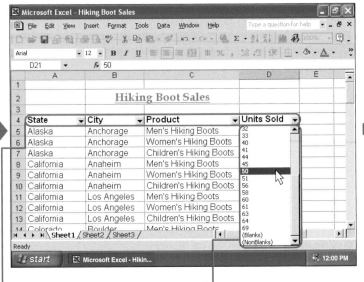

■ An arrow (▼) appears beside each column label.

5 Click ▼ in the column containing the data you want to use to filter the list.

6 Click the data you want to use to filter the list.

How can I use the (Blanks) and (NonBlanks) options to filter my list?

The (Blanks) and (NonBlanks) options are available when you filter a list using a column that contains blank cells. You can select the (Blanks) option to display only the records containing blank cells. You can select the (NonBlanks) option to display only the records without blank cells.

How do I turn off the AutoFilter feature when I no longer want to filter my list?

To turn off the AutoFilter feature, repeat steps 2 to 4 on page 190.

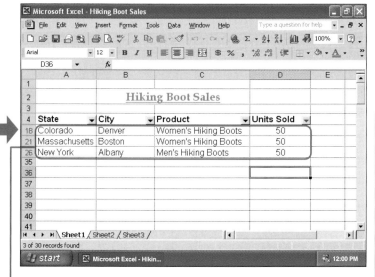

■ The list displays only the records containing the data you specified. The other records are temporarily hidden.

■ In this example, the list displays only the records for stores that sold 50 units.

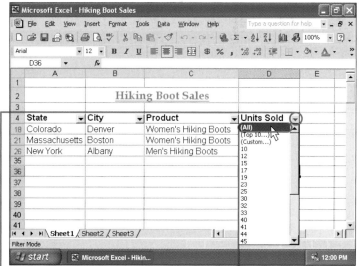

REDISPLAY ALL RECORDS

1 To once again display all the records, click ⬇ in the column containing the data you used to filter the list.

2 Click **(All)**.

CONTINUED ▶

191

You can filter your list to display only records containing data within a specific range.

For example, you can display records for employees whose sales are greater than or equal to $500.

FILTER A LIST BY COMPARING DATA

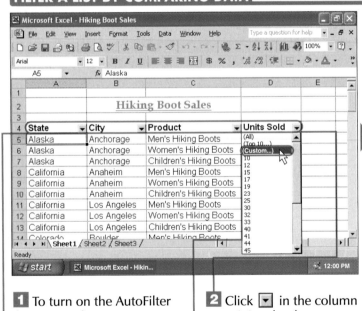

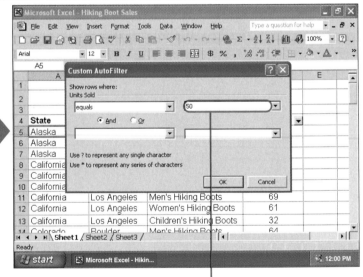

1 To turn on the AutoFilter feature, perform steps 1 to 4 on page 190.

■ An arrow (▼) appears beside each column label.

2 Click ▼ in the column containing the data you want to use to filter the list.

3 Click (**Custom...**).

■ The Custom AutoFilter dialog box appears.

4 Type the data you want Excel to compare to each record in the list.

How can I compare data in my list?

Excel offers many ways you can compare data to help you analyze the data in your list.

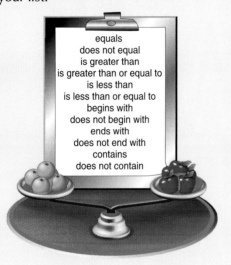

equals
does not equal
is greater than
is greater than or equal to
is less than
is less than or equal to
begins with
does not begin with
ends with
does not end with
contains
does not contain

Can I save the filtered view of my list?

To save the filtered view of your list, save your workbook while the filtered view is displayed. The next time you open your workbook, Excel will display the filtered view of your list. To save a workbook, see page 24.

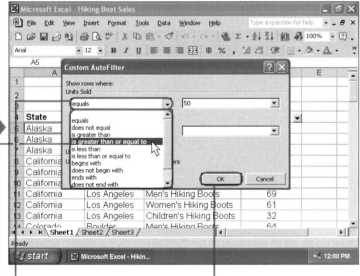

5 Click this area to select how you want Excel to compare the data.

6 Click the way you want Excel to compare the data.

7 Click **OK** to filter the list.

■ The list displays only the records containing the data you specified. The other records are temporarily hidden.

■ In this example, the list displays only the records for stores that sold 50 units or more.

■ To once again display all the records, perform steps 1 and 2 on page 191.

■ To turn off the AutoFilter feature, perform steps 2 to 4 on page 190.

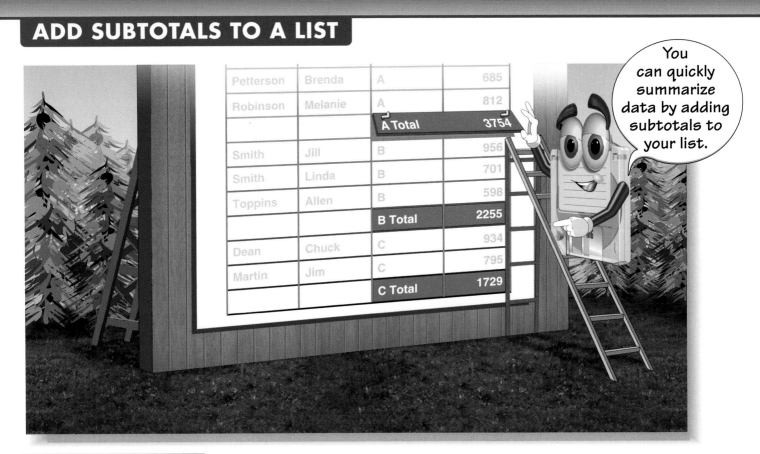

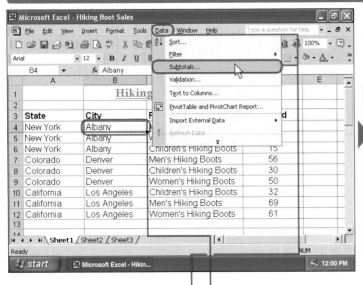

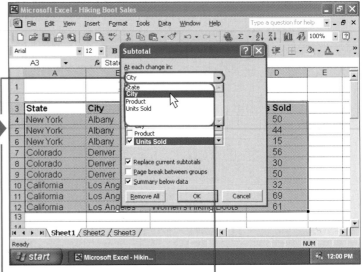

1 Sort the data in the list by the column you want to display subtotals for. To sort data, see page 186.

Note: In this example, the data is sorted by the City column.

2 Click a cell in the list.

3 Click **Data**.

4 Click **Subtotals**.

■ The Subtotal dialog box appears.

5 Click this area to select the column you want to display subtotals for.

6 Click the name of the column you want to display subtotals for.

Note: The column you select should be the same column you sorted data by in step 1.

194

How can subtotals help me?

Subtotals can help you analyze the data in your list. For example, in a list containing department names and sales figures, you can use subtotals to find the total sales for each department and the grand total of all the sales.

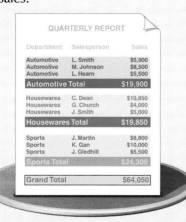

What happens to the subtotals if I change the data in my list?

If you change the data in your list, Excel will automatically recalculate the subtotals and grand total for you.

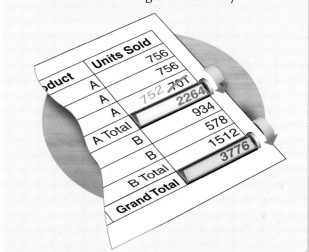

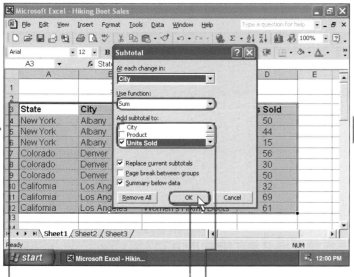

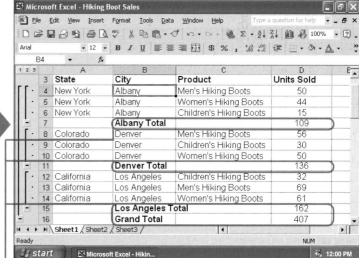

■ This area displays the calculation Excel will perform. You can click this area to select a different calculation.

■ This area displays a check mark (✔) beside each column Excel will subtotal. You can click the box beside a column to add (✔) or remove (☐) a check mark.

7 Click **OK** to add the subtotals to the list.

■ The list displays the subtotals and a grand total.

CONTINUED

ADD SUBTOTALS TO A LIST

After adding subtotals to your list, you can create a subtotal summary report that displays just the grand total, the subtotals and the grand total or all the data in the list.

GRAND TOTAL

Last Name	First Name	Product	Units Sold
		Grand Total	8316

SUBTOTALS & GRAND TOTAL

Last Name	First Name	Product	Units Sold
		A Total	3754
		B Total	2255
		C Total	2307
		Grand Total	8316

ALL THE DATA

Last Name	First Name	Product	Units Sold
Marcuson	Jason	A	632
Matthews	Kathleen	A	1625
Petterson	Brenda	A	685
Robinson	Melanie	A	812
		A Total	3754
Smith	Jill	B	956
Smith	Linda	B	701
Toppins	Allen	B	598
		B Total	2255
Dean	Chuck	C	934
Martin	Jim	C	795
Smith	Michael	C	578
		C Total	2307
		Grand Total	8316

CREATE A SUBTOTAL SUMMARY REPORT

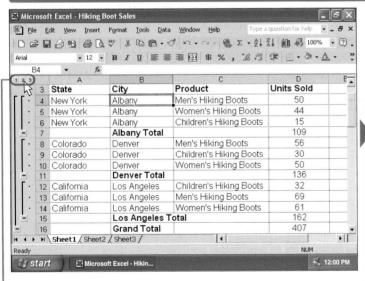

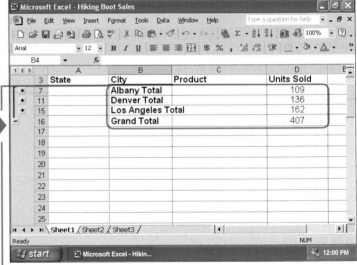

1 Click one of the following buttons to create a subtotal summary report.

- 1 Display only grand total
- 2 Display subtotals and grand total
- 3 Display all the data

■ The subtotal summary report appears, displaying the information you specified. In this example, the other data in the list is temporarily hidden.

Why do plus (➕) and minus (➖) signs appear in the worksheet after I add subtotals to my list?

The plus and minus signs allow you to display and hide subtotaled data.

■ Click a plus sign (➕) to display hidden data.

■ Click a minus sign (➖) to hide data.

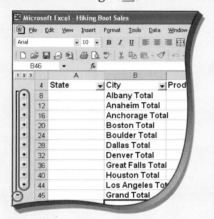

Can I create a chart based on the subtotals in my list?

Yes. Perform step 1 on page 196, selecting ② to display the subtotals and grand total in the list. You can then create a chart to graphically illustrate the subtotals. To create a chart, see page 148.

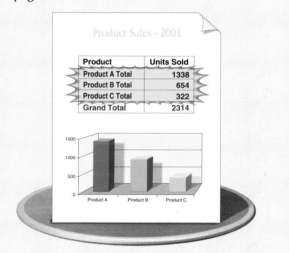

REMOVE SUBTOTALS

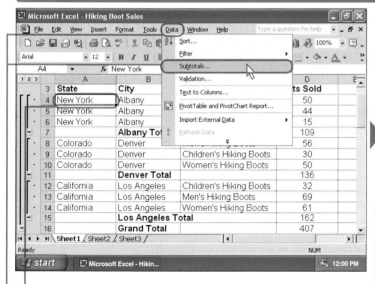

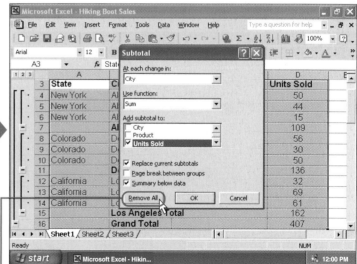

1 Click a cell in the list.

2 Click **Data**.

3 Click **Subtotals**.

■ The Subtotal dialog box appears.

4 Click **Remove All** to remove the subtotals from the list.

■ Excel removes the subtotals from the list.

I am using Office Speech Recognition.
I am using Office Speech Recognition.

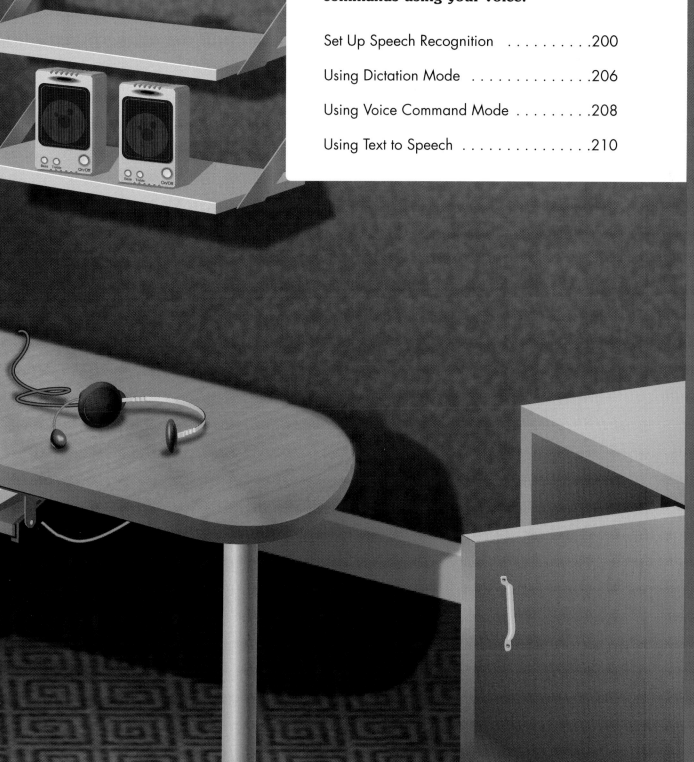

CHAPTER 12

USING SPEECH RECOGNITION

Would you like to use your voice to enter data into a worksheet? Read this chapter to learn how to enter data and select commands using your voice.

Speech recognition allows you to use your voice to enter data into a worksheet and select commands from menus and toolbars. Before you can use speech recognition, you must set up the feature on your computer.

You can set up speech recognition in Microsoft Word, a word processing program included in the Microsoft Office XP suite. Once speech recognition is set up, the feature will be available in Excel.

Before setting up speech recognition, make sure your microphone and speakers are connected to your computer.

SET UP SPEECH RECOGNITION

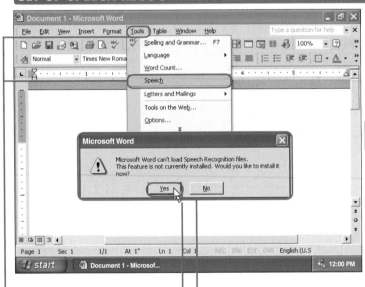

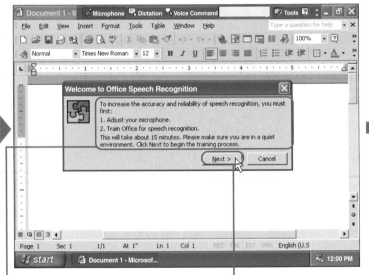

1 To start Microsoft Word, perform steps **1** to **3** on page 6, selecting **Microsoft Word** in step **3**.

2 Click **Tools**.

3 Click **Speech**.

■ A message appears, stating that speech recognition is not currently installed.

4 Insert the CD-ROM disc you used to install Microsoft Office XP into your computer's CD-ROM drive.

5 Click **Yes** to install speech recognition on your computer.

■ When the installation is complete, the Welcome to Office Speech Recognition dialog box appears.

■ This area describes the process of setting up speech recognition on your computer.

6 To begin setting up speech recognition, click **Next**.

Why does this dialog box appear when I try to set up speech recognition?

This dialog box appears if your computer does not meet the minimum hardware requirements needed to use speech recognition. You cannot set up speech recognition if your computer does not meet the minimum hardware requirements.

What type of microphone should I use with speech recognition?

You should use a headset microphone, since this type of microphone will remain in the correct position, even when you move your head. For best results, you should position the microphone approximately one inch from the side of your mouth so that you are not breathing directly into the microphone.

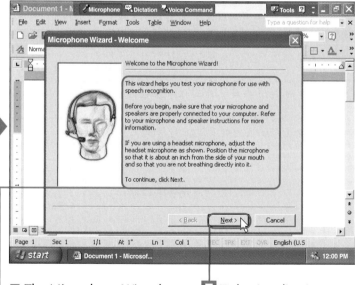

■ The Microphone Wizard appears. The wizard will help you adjust your microphone for use with speech recognition.

■ This area describes the wizard and provides instructions for positioning your microphone.

7 To begin adjusting your microphone, click **Next**.

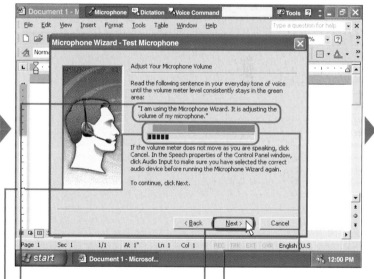

8 Read the text displayed in this area aloud to adjust the volume of your microphone.

■ As you read the text aloud, the volume meter in this area indicates the volume of your microphone.

9 Repeat step 8 until the volume level of your microphone consistently appears in the green area of the volume meter.

10 Click **Next** to continue.

CONTINUED ➤

You can train speech recognition to recognize how you speak. The Microsoft Speech Recognition Training Wizard takes you step by step through the process of training speech recognition.

You can listen to a sample sentence to hear how you should speak during the training.

SET UP SPEECH RECOGNITION (CONTINUED)

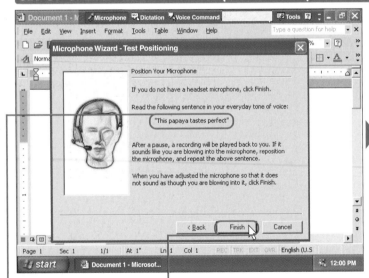

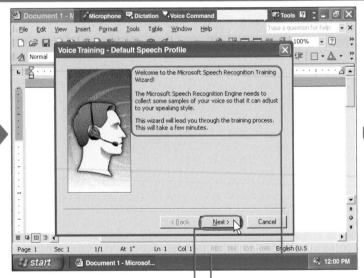

11 Read this text aloud to test the position of your microphone.

■ After a few moments, your voice will be played back to you. If it sounds like you are blowing into the microphone, adjust your microphone's position and then repeat step 11.

12 When you finish positioning your microphone, click **Finish**.

■ The Microsoft Speech Recognition Training Wizard appears. The wizard will help you train speech recognition to recognize how you speak.

■ This area describes the wizard.

13 To begin training speech recognition to recognize how you speak, click **Next**.

Do I have to train speech recognition?

Yes. If you do not train speech recognition, the feature will not work properly. During the training, the Microsoft Speech Recognition Training Wizard gathers information about your voice. The speech recognition feature uses this information to recognize the words you say when entering data or selecting commands.

How should I speak during the training process?

You should speak in your everyday tone of voice, pronouncing words clearly and not pausing between words. You should also speak at a consistent speed.

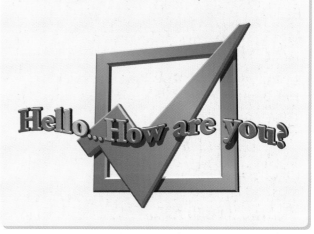

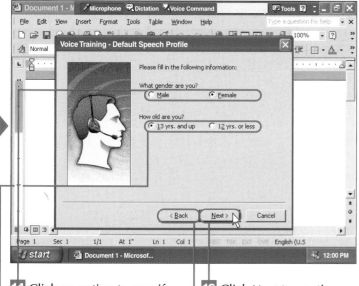

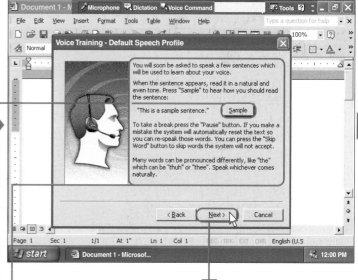

14 Click an option to specify whether you are male or female (○ changes to ⊙).

15 Click an option to indicate your age (○ changes to ⊙).

16 Click **Next** to continue.

■ You can click **Back** to return to a previous step.

■ This area describes the training process.

17 To hear a sample of how you should speak during the training, click **Sample**.

18 Click **Next** to continue.

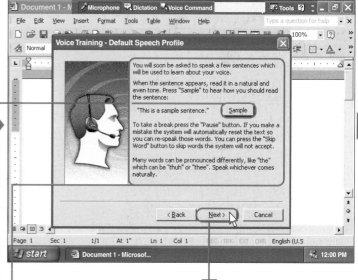

CONTINUED ▶

The Microsoft Speech Recognition Training Wizard provides text you can read aloud to train speech recognition.

You should train speech recognition in a quiet area so that background noise does not interfere with the sound of your voice.

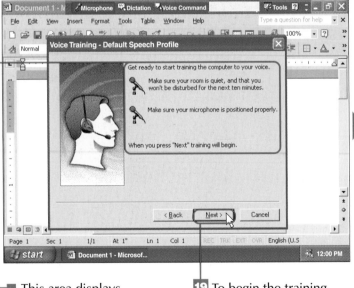

■ This area displays instructions about preparing for the training.

19 To begin the training, click **Next**.

■ The wizard will display a series of screens containing text for you to read aloud.

20 Read the text displayed in this area of each screen.

■ As you read aloud, the wizard highlights the words it recognizes.

■ If the wizard does not recognize a word, it stops highlighting text. If this happens, begin reading again, starting with the first word that is not highlighted.

I have repeated a word several times, but the wizard still does not recognize the word. What should I do?

If the wizard cannot recognize a word you say, you can click the **Skip Word** button to move on to the next word.

Can I perform more training?

The speech recognition feature provides additional training sessions you can perform to improve the accuracy of speech recognition.

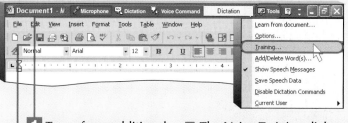

1 To perform additional training, click **Tools** on the Language bar.

2 Click **Training**.

■ The Voice Training dialog box will appear, displaying the available training sessions. Select a training session and then perform steps **18** to **22** starting on page 203.

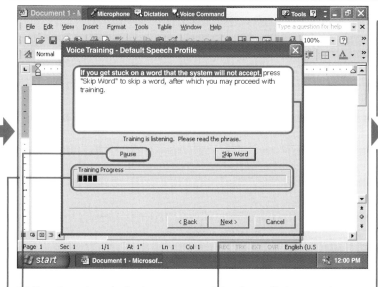

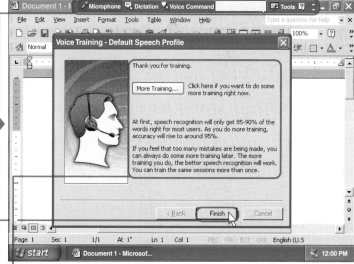

■ To take a break during the training, click **Pause**.

*Note: To resume the training, click **Resume**.*

■ This area displays the progress of the training.

■ When all the text in this area is highlighted, the wizard automatically displays the next screen of text.

21 Repeat step **20** until you have read all the training text.

■ This message appears when the training is complete.

22 Click **Finish** to close the wizard.

■ This area displays the Language bar, which contains buttons you can use to perform tasks using speech recognition.

■ You can now use speech recognition in Excel.

Note: A window will appear, displaying a video that introduces you to speech recognition. When the video is finished, click ⊠ to close the window.

Once you have set up speech recognition, you can use Dictation mode to enter data into a worksheet using your voice.

Speech recognition is designed to be used along with your mouse and keyboard. You can use your voice to enter data into a worksheet and then use your mouse and keyboard to edit the data you entered.

USING DICTATION MODE

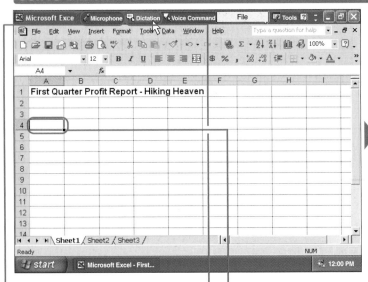

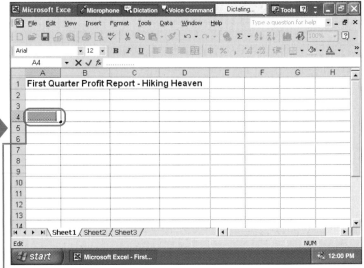

1 If your microphone is turned off, click **Microphone** on the Language bar to turn on the microphone.

Note: When your microphone is turned on, the Dictation and Voice Command buttons appear on the Language bar.

2 Click a cell where you want to enter data using your voice.

3 Click **Dictation** to turn on Dictation mode.

4 Speak into your microphone to enter data into the cell.

■ As you speak, a blue bar appears on the screen to indicate that the computer is processing your voice. You can continue to speak while the blue bar is displayed on the screen.

■ You should not use your mouse or keyboard while the blue bar is displayed on the screen.

What are some of the symbols I can enter using my voice?

To enter:	Say:
=	"Equals"
+	"Plus sign"
%	"Percent sign"
$	"Dollar sign"
>	"Greater than"
<	"Less than"
(	"Open parenthesis"
)	"Close parenthesis"

How should I speak when using speech recognition?

You should speak to your computer in your everyday tone of voice, pronouncing words clearly and not pausing between words. You should also speak at a consistent speed. If you speak too quickly or too slowly, the computer may not be able to recognize what you say.

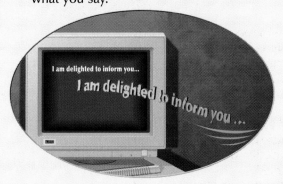

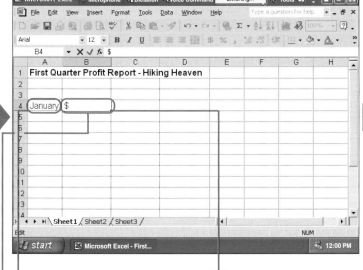

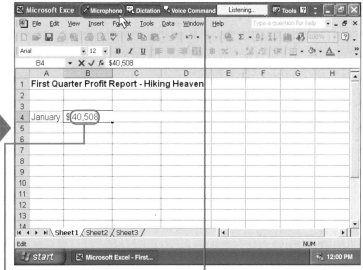

■ As the computer processes your voice, words appear on the screen.

5 To enter data into another cell using your voice, click the cell.

6 To enter a symbol, say the name of the symbol.

Note: For a list of symbols you can enter, see the top of this page.

7 To enter a number, say the number you want to enter.

Note: Numbers less than 20 are entered as words. Numbers greater than 20 are entered as digits.

8 When you finish entering data using your voice, click **Microphone** to turn off your microphone.

■ You can now edit the data you entered using your voice as you would edit any data. To edit data, see page 36.

207

USING VOICE COMMAND MODE

You can use Voice Command mode to select commands from menus and toolbars using your voice.

You can also use Voice Command mode to select options in dialog boxes.

USING VOICE COMMAND MODE

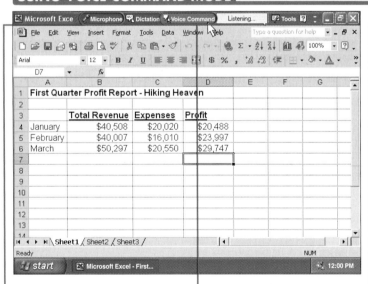

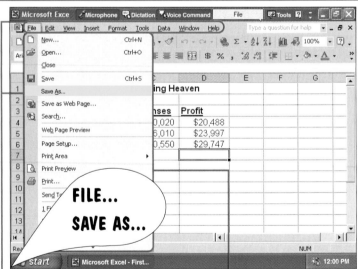

1 If your microphone is turned off, click **Microphone** on the Language bar to turn on the microphone.

Note: When your microphone is turned on, the Dictation and Voice Command buttons appear on the Language bar.

2 Click **Voice Command** to turn on Voice Command mode.

SELECT MENU COMMANDS

1 To select a command from a menu, say the name of the menu.

■ A short version of the menu appears, displaying the most commonly used commands.

Note: To expand the menu and display all the commands, say "expand."

2 To select a command from the menu, say the name of the command.

■ To close a menu without selecting a command, say "escape."

208

Can I use Voice Command mode to select an option in a task pane?

Yes. Task panes display links that allow you to perform common tasks. To select a link in a task pane using your voice, say the full name of the link. For more information on task panes, see page 18.

Can I use Voice Command mode to perform other tasks?

In addition to selecting commands, you can use Voice Command mode to change the active cell.

To:	Say:
Move down one cell	"Down" or "Enter"
Move up one cell	"Up"
Move left one cell	"Left"
Move right one cell	"Right"

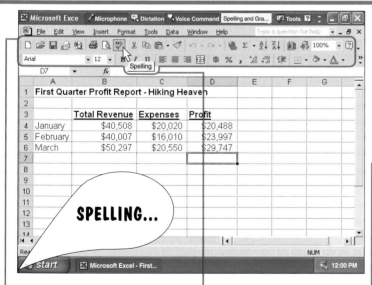

SELECT TOOLBAR COMMANDS

■1 To select a command from a toolbar, say the name of the toolbar button.

■ To determine the name of a toolbar button, position the mouse over the button. After a few seconds, the name of the button appears in a yellow box.

SELECT DIALOG BOX OPTIONS

■ A dialog box may appear when you select a menu or toolbar command.

■1 To select an option in a dialog box, say the name of the option.

■ If the dialog box contains tabs, you can say the name of a tab to display the tab.

■2 When you finish selecting commands using your voice, click **Microphone** to turn off your microphone.

Before using the text to speech feature, make sure your speakers are connected to your computer.

USING TEXT TO SPEECH

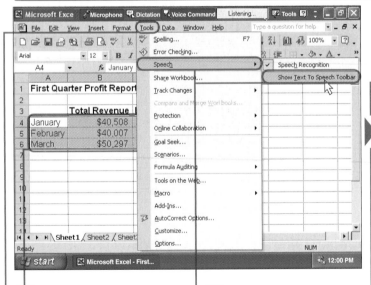

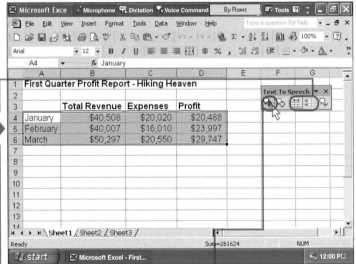

1 Select the cells containing the data you want your computer to read back to you. To select cells, see page 12.

2 Click **Tools**.

3 Click **Speech**.

Note: If Speech does not appear on the menu, position the mouse over the bottom of the menu to display all the menu options.

4 Click **Show Text To Speech Toolbar**.

■ The Text To Speech toolbar appears.

5 Click a button to specify how you want your computer to read data back to you.

⊞ Read data by rows

⊞ Read data by columns

6 Click 🔁 to have your computer read the data in the selected cells back to you.

How can I have my computer read data back to me as I enter data into cells?

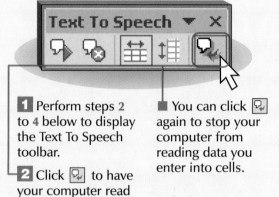

1 Perform steps **2** to **4** below to display the Text To Speech toolbar.

2 Click 🖳 to have your computer read data back to you as you enter data into cells.

■ You can click 🖳 again to stop your computer from reading data you enter into cells.

Will my computer read data in hidden rows or columns?

No. Your computer will not read data in hidden rows or columns. For information on hiding rows and columns, see page 84.

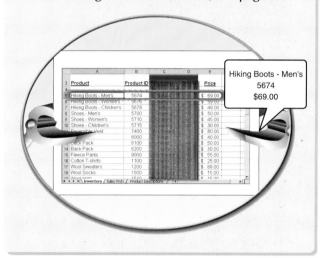

Hiking Boots - Men's
5674
$69.00

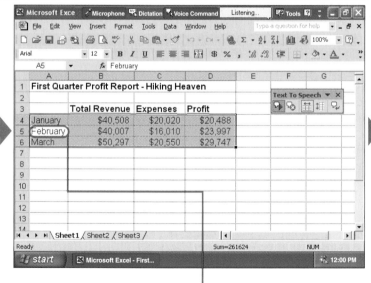

■ Your computer reads the data in the selected cells.

■ The cell your computer is currently reading is highlighted.

■ To stop your computer from reading data back to you, click 🖳.

Note: You can click ▶ to once again have your computer read data back to you.

7 When your computer finishes reading data back to you, click ⊠ to hide the Text To Speech toolbar.

EXCEL AND THE INTERNET

Are you wondering how you can use
Excel to share data with other people
on the Internet? In this chapter, you will
learn how to e-mail a worksheet, save
a workbook as a Web page and more.

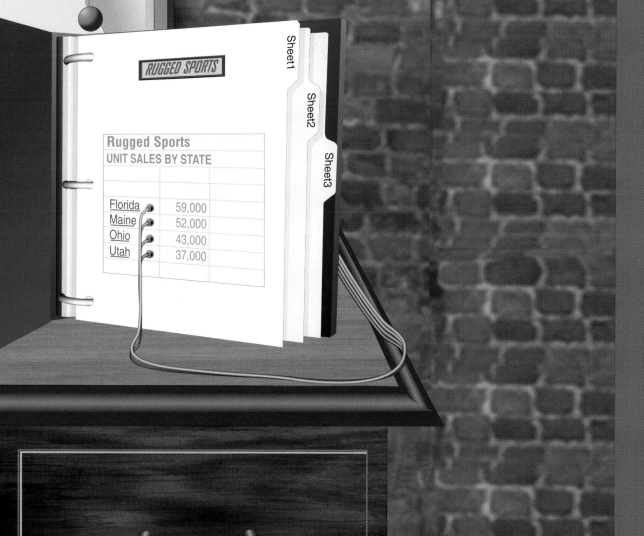

You can e-mail the worksheet displayed on your screen to a friend, family member or colleague.

Before you can e-mail a worksheet, an e-mail program such as Microsoft Outlook must be set up on your computer.

E-MAIL A WORKSHEET

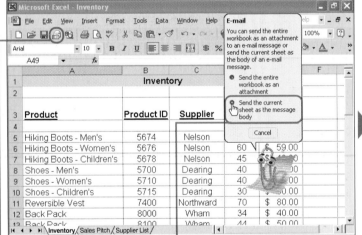

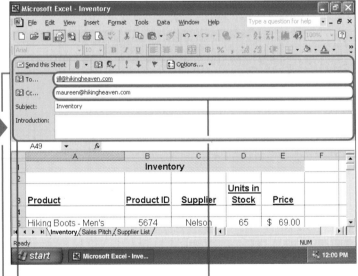

1 Click 🖃 to e-mail the current worksheet.

Note: If 🖃 is not displayed, click ≫ on the Standard toolbar to display the button.

■ If the workbook contains data on more than one worksheet, a message appears, asking if you want to send the entire workbook or just the current worksheet.

2 Click this option to send the current worksheet.

■ An area appears for you to address the message.

3 Click this area and type the e-mail address of the person you want to receive the message.

4 To send a copy of the message to a person who is not directly involved but would be interested in the message, click this area and type their e-mail address.

Note: To enter more than one e-mail address in step 3 or 4, separate each e-mail address with a semi-colon (;).

Why would I include an introduction for a worksheet I am sending in an e-mail message?

Including an introduction allows you to provide the recipient of the message with additional information about the worksheet. For example, the recipient may require instructions or an explanation of the content of the worksheet.

How do I e-mail an entire workbook?

To e-mail an entire workbook, perform steps 1 to 5 below, selecting **Send the entire workbook as an attachment** in step 2. Then click **Send** to send the message. When you e-mail an entire workbook, the workbook is sent as an attached file.

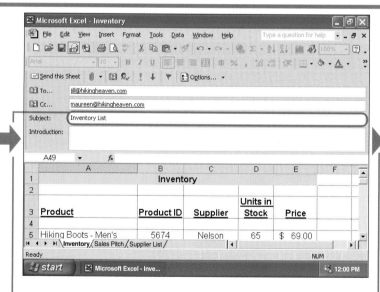

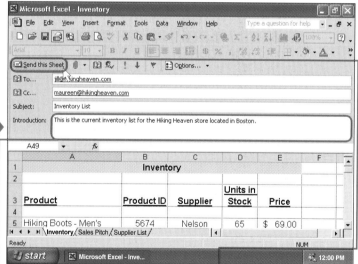

5 Click this area and type a subject for the message.

Note: If a subject already exists, you can drag the mouse I over the existing subject and then type a new subject.

6 To include an introduction for the worksheet you are sending, click this area and type the introduction.

Note: You can include an introduction only if you are using the Microsoft Outlook e-mail program.

7 Click **Send this Sheet** to send the message.

Note: If you are not currently connected to the Internet, a dialog box will appear allowing you to connect.

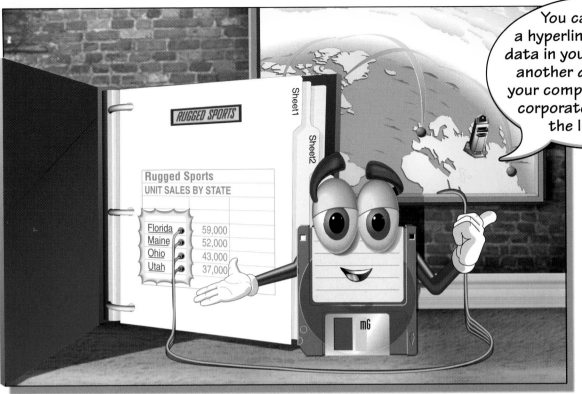

You can create a hyperlink to connect data in your workbook to another document on your computer, network, corporate intranet or the Internet.

An intranet is a small version of the Internet within a company or organization.

You can easily identify hyperlinks in your workbook. Hyperlinks appear underlined and in color.

CREATE A HYPERLINK

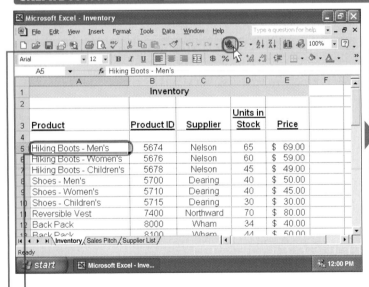

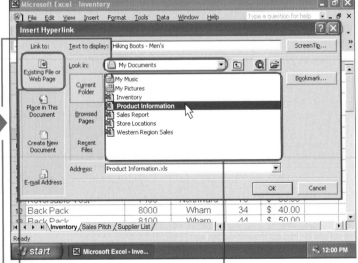

1 Select the cells containing the data you want to make a hyperlink. To select cells, see page 12.

2 Click 🔗 to create a hyperlink.

Note: If 🔗 is not displayed, click ≫ on the Standard toolbar to display the button.

■ The Insert Hyperlink dialog box appears.

3 Click **Existing File or Web Page** to link the data to an existing document.

■ This area shows the location of the displayed documents. You can click this area to change the location.

4 To link the data to a document on your computer or network, click the document in this area.

Can I select a cell that contains a hyperlink?

Yes. Excel allows you to select a cell that contains a hyperlink without displaying the document or Web page connected to the hyperlink. This is useful when you want to change the format of a hyperlink. To select a cell that contains a hyperlink, position the mouse 👆 over the cell and then hold down the left mouse button until the mouse 👆 changes to ⊹.

Can Excel automatically create a hyperlink for me?

When you type the address of a document located on your network or the Internet, Excel will automatically change the address to a hyperlink for you.

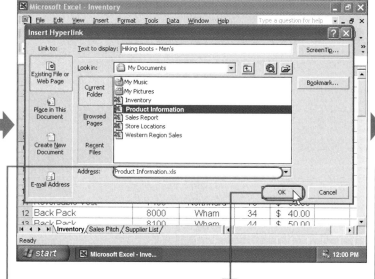

■ To link the data to a page on the Web, click this area and then type the address of the Web page (example: www.maran.com).

5 Click **OK** to create the hyperlink.

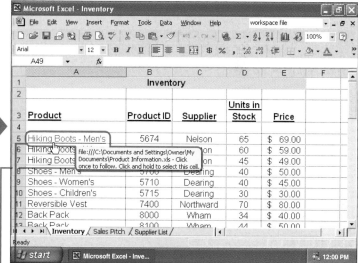

■ Excel creates the hyperlink. Hyperlinks appear underlined and in color.

■ When you position the mouse 👆 over a hyperlink, a yellow box appears, indicating where the hyperlink will take you.

■ You can click the hyperlink to display the document or Web page connected to the hyperlink.

Note: If the hyperlink connects to a Web page, your Web browser will open and display the page.

PREVIEW A WORKBOOK AS A WEB PAGE

You can preview how your workbook will look as a Web page. This allows you to see how the workbook will appear on the Internet or your company's intranet.

An intranet is a small version of the Internet within a company or organization.

PREVIEW A WORKBOOK AS A WEB PAGE

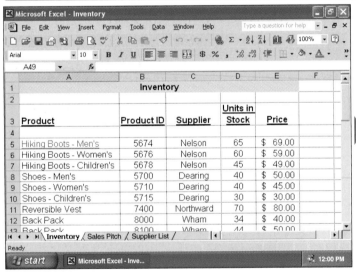

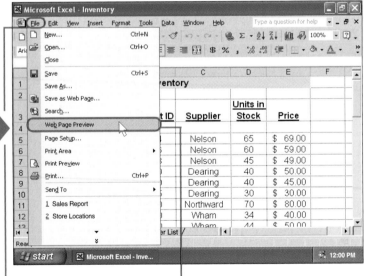

1 Open the workbook you want to preview as a Web page. To open a workbook, see page 30.

2 Click **File**.

3 Click **Web Page Preview** to preview your workbook as a Web page.

Will my Web page look the same when displayed in different Web browsers?

No. Different Web browsers may display your Web page differently. There are many Web browsers used on the Web. The two most popular Web browsers are Microsoft Internet Explorer and Netscape Navigator.

Microsoft Internet Explorer

Netscape Navigator

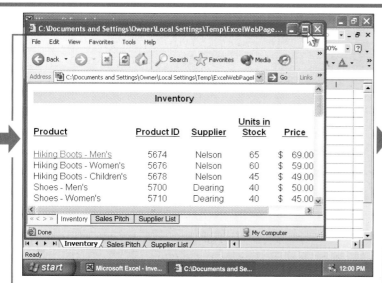

■ Your Web browser window opens, displaying your workbook as a Web page.

4 To maximize the Web browser window to fill your screen, click 🗖.

■ The gridlines that separate each cell do not appear in the Web browser window.

■ If your workbook contains data on more than one worksheet, this area displays a tab for each worksheet.

5 To display the contents of a different worksheet, click a tab.

6 When you finish previewing your workbook as a Web page, click ✕ to close the Web browser window.

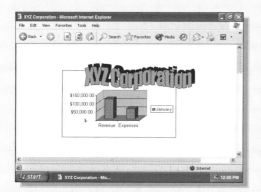

You can save a workbook as a Web page. This allows you to place the workbook on the Internet or your company's intranet.

An intranet is a small version of the Internet within a company or organization.

SAVE A WORKBOOK AS A WEB PAGE

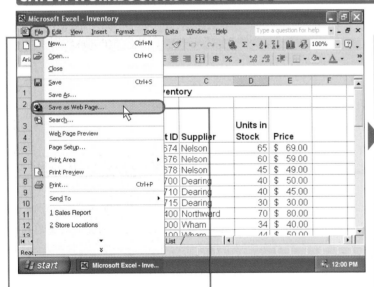

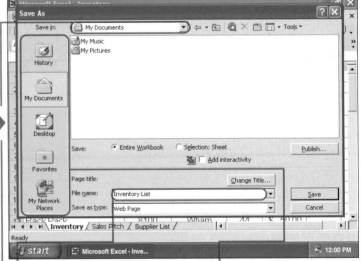

1 Open the workbook you want to save as a Web page. To open a workbook, see page 30.

2 Click **File**.

3 Click **Save as Web Page**.

■ The Save As dialog box appears.

4 Type a file name for the Web page.

■ This area shows the location where Excel will store the Web page. You can click this area to change the location.

■ This area allows you to access commonly used locations. You can click a location to save the Web page in the location.

Note: For information on the commonly used locations, see the top of page 25.

What is the difference between the file name and the title of a Web page?

The file name is the name you use to store the Web page on your computer. The title is the text that will appear at the top of the Web browser window when a person views your Web page.

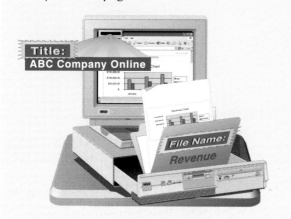

How do I make my Web page available for other people to view?

After you save your workbook as a Web page, you can transfer the page to a computer that stores Web pages, called a Web server. Once the Web page is stored on a Web server, the page will be available for other people to view. For information on transferring a Web page to a Web server, contact your network administrator or Internet service provider.

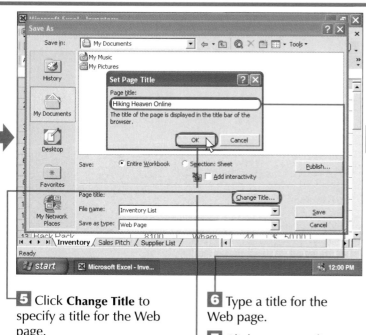

5 Click **Change Title** to specify a title for the Web page.

■ The Set Page Title dialog box appears.

6 Type a title for the Web page.

7 Click **OK** to confirm the title.

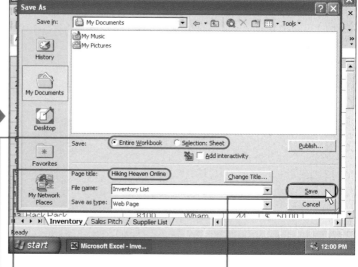

■ This area displays the title you specified for the Web page.

8 Click an option to specify whether you want to save the entire workbook or just the current worksheet as a Web page (○ changes to ⊙).

9 Click **Save** to save the Web page.

INDEX

INDEX

Search task pane, 19
select
    cells, 12-13
    columns, 13
    commands, 16-17
        using menus, 16-17
        using toolbars, 16-17
    dialog box options, using Voice Command mode, 209
    hyperlinks, 217
    menu commands, using Voice Command mode, 208
    rows, 13
    task pane options, using Voice Command mode, 209
    toolbar commands, using Voice Command mode, 209
series, complete, 14-15
servers, Web, 221
set print area, 116-117
set up, speech recognition, 200-205
shapes, add to diagrams, 178-179
size
    charts, 153
    data, 91, 94-95
    objects, 173
    of printed data, change, 128-129
smart tags
    turn on, 54-55
    using, 56-57
sort, data in lists, 186-189
speech recognition
    Dictation mode, using, 206-207
    overview, 5
    set up, 200-205
    text to speech, using, 210-211
    training, 202-205
    Voice Command mode, using, 208-209
spelling, check, 42-43
spreadsheets. *See* Excel; worksheets
Standard toolbar
    as part of the Excel window, 7
start. *See also* open
    Excel, 6
status bar, as part of the Excel window, 7
stock prices, refresh, 55
stop repeating labels on printed pages, 131
strikethrough effect, 95
subscript effect, 95
subtotal summary report, create, 196-197
subtotals
    add to lists, 194-195
    create charts using, 197
    display or hide, 196
    remove from lists, 197

subtraction. *See* formulas; functions
Sum
    common calculation, 69
    function, 61
summarize data in lists, 194-195
superscript effect, 95
switch between
    workbooks, 27
    worksheets, 134

T

tabs, worksheets, 7
    browse through, 134
    color, 139
target diagrams, 177
task pane
    as part of the Excel window, 7
    use, 18-19
        to open workbooks, 31
text
    add
        to AutoShapes, 165
        to diagrams, 177
    check spelling, 42-43
    edit
        in text boxes, 167
        in WordArt, 163
    wrap in cells, 100-101
text boxes, 166-167
    check spelling, 43
text series, complete, 14-15
text to speech, using, 210-211
title bar, as part of the Excel window, 7
titles on charts, 149
    change, 156
toolbars
    buttons, move or copy data using, 41
    commands, select using Voice Command mode, 209
    display or hide, 82
    move, 83
    select commands using, 16-17
training, speech recognition, 202-205
turn on smart tags, 54-55

U

underline data, 92, 94-95
undo changes, 39
unfreeze rows and columns, 87

Read Less – Learn More™

Visual

with these full-color Visual™ guides

The Fast and Easy Way to Learn

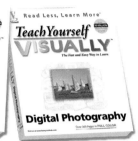

Discover how to use what you learn with "Teach Yourself" tips

Title	ISBN	U.S. Price
Teach Yourself Access 97 VISUALLY™	0-7645-6026-3	$29.99
Teach Yourself FrontPage® 2000 VISUALLY™	0-7645-3451-3	$29.99
Teach Yourself HTML VISUALLY™	0-7645-3423-8	$29.99
Teach Yourself the Internet and World Wide Web VISUALLY™, 2nd Ed.	0-7645-3410-6	$29.99
Teach Yourself Microsoft® Access 2000 VISUALLY™	0-7645-6059-X	$29.99
Teach Yourself Microsoft® Excel 97 VISUALLY™	0-7645-6063-8	$29.99
Teach Yourself Microsoft® Excel 2000 VISUALLY™	0-7645-6056-5	$29.99
Teach Yourself Microsoft® Office 2000 VISUALLY™	0-7645-6051-4	$29.99
Teach Yourself Microsoft® PowerPoint® 97 VISUALLY™	0-7645-6062-X	$29.99
Teach Yourself Microsoft® PowerPoint® 2000 VISUALLY™	0-7645-6060-3	$29.99
Teach Yourself Microsoft® Word 2000 VISUALLY™	0-7645-6055-7	$29.99
Teach Yourself More Windows® 98 VISUALLY™	0-7645-6044-1	$29.99
Teach Yourself Office 97 VISUALLY™	0-7645-6018-2	$29.99
Teach Yourself Red Hat® Linux® VISUALLY™	0-7645-3430-0	$29.99
Teach Yourself VISUALLY™ Computers, 3rd Ed.	0-7645-3525-0	$29.99
Teach Yourself VISUALLY™ Digital Photography	0-7645-3565-X	$29.99
Teach Yourself VISUALLY™ Dreamweaver® 3	0-7645-3470-X	$29.99
Teach Yourself VISUALLY™ Dreamweaver® 4	0-7645-0851-2	$29.99
Teach Yourself VISUALLY™ E-commerce With FrontPage®	0-7645-3579-X	$29.99
Teach Yourself VISUALLY™ Excel 2002	0-7645-3594-3	$29.99
Teach Yourself VISUALLY™ Fireworks® 4	0-7645-3566-8	$29.99
Teach Yourself VISUALLY™ Flash™ 5	0-7645-3540-4	$29.99
Teach Yourself VISUALLY™ FrontPage® 2002	0-7645-3590-0	$29.99
Teach Yourself VISUALLY™ iMac™	0-7645-3453-X	$29.99
Teach Yourself VISUALLY™ Investing Online	0-7645-3459-9	$29.99
Teach Yourself VISUALLY™ Networking, 2nd Ed.	0-7645-3534-X	$29.99
Teach Yourself VISUALLY™ Office XP	0-7645-0854-7	$29.99
Teach Yourself VISUALLY™ Photoshop® 6	0-7645-3513-7	$29.99
Teach Yourself VISUALLY™ Quicken® 2001	0-7645-3526-9	$29.99
Teach Yourself VISUALLY™ Windows® 2000 Server	0-7645-3428-9	$29.99
Teach Yourself VISUALLY™ Windows® Me Millennium Edition	0-7645-3495-5	$29.99
Teach Yourself VISUALLY™ Windows® XP	0-7645-3619-2	$29.99
Teach Yourself Windows® 95 VISUALLY™	0-7645-6001-8	$29.99
Teach Yourself Windows® 98 VISUALLY™	0-7645-6025-5	$29.99
Teach Yourself Windows® 2000 Professional VISUALLY™	0-7645-6040-9	$29.99
Teach Yourself Windows NT® 4 VISUALLY™	0-7645-6061-1	$29.99
Teach Yourself Word 97 VISUALLY™	0-7645-6032-8	$29.99

TRADE & INDIVIDUAL ORDERS

Phone: **(800) 762-2974**
or **(317) 572-3993**
(8 a.m.–6 p.m., CST, weekdays)
FAX : **(800) 550-2747**
or **(317) 572-4002**

EDUCATIONAL ORDERS & DISCOUNTS

Phone: **(800) 434-2086**
(8:30 a.m.–5:00 p.m., CST, weekdays)
FAX : **(317) 572-4005**

CORPORATE ORDERS FOR VISUAL™ SERIES

Phone: **(800) 469-6616**
(8:30 a.m.–5 p.m., EST, weekdays)
FAX : **(905) 890-9434**

Qty	ISBN	Title	Price	Total

Shipping & Handling Charges

	Description	First book	Each add'l. book	Total
Domestic	Normal	$4.50	$1.50	$
	Two Day Air	$8.50	$2.50	$
	Overnight	$18.00	$3.00	$
International	Surface	$8.00	$8.00	$
	Airmail	$16.00	$16.00	$
	DHL Air	$17.00	$17.00	$

Subtotal _____

CA residents add
applicable sales tax _____

IN, MA and MD
residents add
5% sales tax _____

IL residents add
6.25% sales tax _____

RI residents add
7% sales tax _____

TX residents add
8.25% sales tax _____

Shipping _____

Total _____

Ship to:

Name _____

Address _____

Company _____

City/State/Zip _____

Daytime Phone _____

Payment: ☐ Check to Hungry Minds (US Funds Only)
☐ Visa ☐ Mastercard ☐ American Express

Card # _____ Exp. _____ Signature _____

Hungry Minds™

maranGraphics®